CATHOLIC
SUNDAY MASS READING(
FOR 2024

**Catholic Sunday Mass Readings For 2024
with the Principal Celebrations of the Liturgical Year B,
in 2024**

Compiled by

Catholic Lectionary Publishers

CONTENTS
Section A
PRINCIPAL CELEBRATIONS OF THE LITURGICAL YEAR B, 2024 - 4
Section B
SUNDAY AND DAILY MASS READINGS FOR 2024 - - - - - - 5

JANUARY -   5 - 12

FEBRUARY-   12 - 19

MARCH - 20 - 39

APRIL - 39 - 47

MAY - 47 - 61

JUNE - 62 - 71

JULY - 72 - 80

AUGUST - 80 - 88

SEPTEMBER - 88 - 98

OCTOBER - 98 - 107

NOVEMBER - 108 - 115

DECEMBER - 115 - 128

SECTION A
PRINCIPAL CELEBRATIONS OF THE LITURGICAL YEAR B, 2024

CELEBRATIONS	DATE
First Sunday of Advent, Year B	December 3, 2023
Ash Wednesday	February 14, 2024
Easter Sunday	March 31, 2024
The Ascension of the Lord	May 12, 2024
Pentecost Sunday	May 19, 2024
The Most Holy Body and Blood of Christ (*Corpus Christi*)	June 16, 2022
First Sunday of Advent, Year C	December 1, 2024

SUNDAY AND DAILY MASS READINGS 2024
Sunday January 7 2024
Solemnity of the Epiphany of the Lord

First Reading: Isaiah 60:1-6

¹Rise up in splendor, Jerusalem! Your light
     has come,
  the glory of the Lord shines upon you.
²See, darkness covers the earth,
  and thick clouds cover the peoples;
but upon you the LORD shines,
  and over you appears his glory.
³Nations shall walk by your light,
  and kings by your shining radiance.
⁴Raise your eyes and look about;
  they all gather and come to you:
your sons come from afar,
  and your daughters in the arms of their
    nurses.

⁵Then you shall be radiant at what you see,
  your heart shall throb and overflow,
for the riches of the sea shall be emptied out
  before you,
  the wealth of nations shall be brought to
  you.
⁶Caravans of camels shall fill you,
  dromedaries from Midian and Ephah;
all from Sheba shall come
  bearing gold and frankincense,
  and proclaiming the praises of the LORD.

Responsorial Psalm: Psalms 72:1-2, 7-8, 10-11, 12-13.

R. *(cf. 11)* **Lord, every nation on earth will adore you.**

¹O God, with your judgment endow the king,
  and with your justice, the king's son;
²He shall govern your people with justice
  and your afflicted ones with judgment.

R. Lord, every nation on earth will adore you.

[7] Justice shall flower in his days,
> and profound peace, till the moon be no
> > more.

[8] May he rule from sea to sea,
> and from the River to the ends of the
> > earth.

R. Lord, every nation on earth will adore you.

[10] The kings of Tarshish and the Isles shall
> > offer gifts;
> the kings of Arabia and Seba shall bring
> > tribute.

[11] All kings shall pay him homage,
> all nations shall serve him.

R. Lord, every nation on earth will adore you.

[12] For he shall rescue the poor when he cries
> > out,
> and the afflicted when he has no one to
> > help him.

[13] He shall have pity for the lowly and the
> > poor;
> the lives of the poor he shall save.

R. Lord, every nation on earth will adore you.

Second Reading: Ephesians 3:2-3A, 5-6

Brothers and sisters: [2]You have heard of the stewardship of God's grace that was given to me for your benefit, [3A]namely, that the mystery was made known to me by revelation. [5]It was not made known to people in other generations as it has now been revealed to his holy apostles and prophets by the Spirit: [6]that the Gentiles are coheirs, members of the same body, and copartners in the promise in Christ Jesus through the gospel.

Alleluia: Matthew 2:2

R. Alleluia, alleluia.
[2]We saw his star at its rising
and have come to do him homage.
R. Alleluia, alleluia.

Gospel: Matthew 2:1-12

[1]When Jesus was born in Bethlehem of Judea, in the days of King Herod, behold, magi from the east arrived in Jerusalem, [2]saying, "Where is the newborn king of the Jews? We saw his star at its rising and have come to do him homage." [3]When King Herod heard this, he was greatly troubled, and all Jerusalem with him. [4]Assembling all the chief priests and the scribes of the people, He inquired of them where the Christ was to be born. [5]They said to him, "In Bethlehem of Judea, for thus it has been written through the prophet:

[6]*And you, Bethlehem, land of Judah,*
>*are by no means least among the rulers of*
>>*Judah;*
since from you shall come a ruler,
>*who is to shepherd my people Israel."*

[7]Then Herod called the magi secretly and ascertained from them the time of the star's appearance. [8]He sent them to Bethlehem and said, "Go and search diligently for the child. When you have found him, bring me word, that I too may go and do him homage." [9]After their audience with the king they set out. And behold, the star that they had seen at its rising preceded them, until it came and stopped over the place where the child was. [10]They were overjoyed at seeing the star, [11]and on entering the house they saw the child with Mary his mother. They prostrated themselves and did him homage. Then they opened their treasures and offered him gifts of gold, frankincense, and myrrh. [12]And having been warned in a dream not to return to Herod, they departed for their country by another way.

Sunday January 14, 2024

Second Sunday in Ordinary Time Year B
First Reading: 1 Samuel 3:3B-10, 19

[3B]Samuel was sleeping in the temple of the LORD where the ark of God was.[4]The LORD called to Samuel, who answered, "Here I am."[5]Samuel ran to Eli and said, "Here I am. You called me." "I did not call you," Eli said. "Go back to sleep." So he went back to sleep.[6]Again the LORD called Samuel, who rose and went to Eli. "Here I am, " he said. "You called me." But Eli answered, "I did not call you, my son. Go back to sleep."

[7]At that time Samuel was not familiar with the LORD, because the LORD had not revealed anything to him as yet. [8]The LORD called Samuel again, for the third time. Getting up and going to Eli, he said, "Here I am. You called me." Then Eli understood that the LORD was calling the youth.[9]So he said to Samuel, "Go to sleep, and if you are called, reply, Speak, LORD, for your servant is listening." When Samuel went to sleep in his place,[10]the LORD came and revealed his presence,

calling out as before, "Samuel, Samuel!" Samuel answered, "Speak, for your servant is listening."

¹⁹Samuel grew up, and the LORD was with him, not permitting any word of his to be without effect.

Responsorial Psalm: Psalms 40:2, 4, 7-8, 8-9, 10

R. *(8a and 9a)* **Here am I, Lord; I come to do your will.**

² I have waited, waited for the LORD,
    and he stooped toward me and heard my
       cry.
^{4AB} And he put a new song into my mouth,
    a hymn to our God.
R. Here am I, Lord; I come to do your will.

⁷ Sacrifice or offering you wished not,
    but ears open to obedience you gave me.
Holocausts or sin-offerings you sought not;
    ^{8A} then said I, "Behold I come."
R. Here I am, Lord; I come to do your will.

^{8B1} "In the written scroll it is prescribed for me,
    ⁹to do your will, O my God, is my delight,
and your law is within my heart!"
R. Here am I, Lord; I come to do your will.
¹⁰ I announced your justice in the vast
       assembly;
    I did not restrain my lips, as you, O LORD,
       know.
R. Here am I, Lord; I come to do your will.

Second Reading: 1 Corinthians 6:13C-15A, 17-20

Brothers and sisters: ^{13C}The body is not for immorality, but for the Lord, and the Lord is for the body; ¹⁴God raised the Lord and will also raise us by his power.

^{15A} Do you not know that your bodies are members of Christ? ¹⁷But whoever is joined to the Lord becomes one Spirit with him.¹⁸Avoid immorality. Every other sin a person commits is outside the body, but the immoral person sins against his own body.¹⁹Do you not know that your body is a temple of the Holy Spirit within you, whom you have from God, and that you are not your own? ²⁰For you have been purchased at a price. Therefore glorify God in your body.

Alleluia: John 1:41, 17B

R. Alleluia, alleluia.

[41] We have found the Messiah:

[17B] Jesus Christ, who brings us truth and grace.

R. Alleluia, alleluia.

Gospel: John 1:35-42

[35]John was standing with two of his disciples,[36]and as he watched Jesus walk by, he said, "Behold, the Lamb of God." [37]The two disciples heard what he said and followed Jesus.[38]Jesus turned and saw them following him and said to them, "What are you looking for?" They said to him, "Rabbi" – which translated means Teacher, "where are you staying?" [39]He said to them, "Come, and you will see." So they went and saw where Jesus was staying, and they stayed with him that day. It was about four in the afternoon.[40]Andrew, the brother of Simon Peter, was one of the two who heard John and followed Jesus. [41]He first found his own brother Simon and told him, "We have found the Messiah" – which is translated Christ. [42]Then he brought him to Jesus. Jesus looked at him and said, "You are Simon the son of John; you will be called Cephas" – which is translated Peter.

Sunday January 21, 2024

Third Sunday in Ordinary Time, Year B

First Reading: Jonah 3:1-5, 10

[1]The word of the LORD came to Jonah, saying: [2]"Set out for the great city of Nineveh, and announce to it the message that I will tell you." [3]So Jonah made ready and went to Nineveh, according to the LORD'S bidding. Now Nineveh was an enormously large city; it took three days to go through it.[4]Jonah began his journey through the city, and had gone but a single day's walk announcing, "Forty days more and Nineveh shall be destroyed," [5]when the people of Nineveh believed God; they proclaimed a fast and all of them, great and small, put on sackcloth.

[10]When God saw by their actions how they turned from their evil way, he repented of the evil that he had threatened to do to them; he did not carry it out.

Responsorial Psalm: Psalms 25:4-5, 6-7, 8-9

R. [4a] Teach me your ways, O Lord.

[4] Your ways, O LORD, make known to me;
　　teach me your paths,

[5] Guide me in your truth and teach me,
　　for you are God my savior.

R. Teach me your ways, O Lord.

⁶ Remember that your compassion, O LORD,
>   and your love are from of old.
⁷ In your kindness remember me,
>   because of your goodness, O LORD.
R. Teach me your ways, O Lord.

⁸ Good and upright is the LORD;
>   thus he shows sinners the way.
⁹ He guides the humble to justice
>   and teaches the humble his way.
R. Teach me your ways, O Lord.

Second Reading: 1 Corinthians 7:29-31

²⁹I tell you, brothers and sisters, the time is running out. From now on, let those having wives act as not having them, ³⁰those weeping as not weeping, those rejoicing as not rejoicing, those buying as not owning,³¹those using the world as not using it fully. For the world in its present form is passing away.

Alleluia: Mark 1:15

R. Alleluia, alleluia.
¹⁵The kingdom of God is at hand.
Repent and believe in the Gospel.
R. Alleluia, alleluia.

Gospel: Mark 1:14-20

¹⁴After John had been arrested, Jesus came to Galilee proclaiming the gospel of God: ¹⁵ "This is the time of fulfillment. The kingdom of God is at hand. Repent, and believe in the gospel."

¹⁶As he passed by the Sea of Galilee, he saw Simon and his brother Andrew casting their nets into the sea; they were fishermen. ¹⁷Jesus said to them, "Come after me, and I will make you fishers of men." ¹⁸Then they abandoned their nets and followed him. ¹⁹He walked along a little farther and saw James, the son of Zebedee, and his brother John. They too were in a boat mending their nets. ²⁰Then he called them. So they left their father Zebedee in the boat along with the hired men and followed him.

Fourth Sunday in Ordinary Time Year B

First Reading: Deuteronomy 18:15-20

Moses spoke to all the people, saying: [15]"A prophet like me will the LORD, your God, raise up for you from among your own kin; to him you shall listen.[16]This is exactly what you requested of the LORD, your God, at Horeb on the day of the assembly, when you said, 'Let us not again hear the voice of the LORD, our God, nor see this great fire any more, lest we die.' [17]And the LORD said to me, 'This was well said. [18]I will raise up for them a prophet like you from among their kin, and will put my words into his mouth; he shall tell them all that I command him.[19]Whoever will not listen to my words which he speaks in my name, I myself will make him answer for it.[20]But if a prophet presumes to speak in my name an oracle that I have not commanded him to speak, or speaks in the name of other gods, he shall die.'"

Responsorial Psalm: Psalms 95:1-2, 6-7, 7-9

R. [8] *If today you hear his voice, harden not your hearts.*

[1] Come, let us sing joyfully to the LORD;
     let us acclaim the rock of our salvation.
[2] Let us come into his presence with
          thanksgiving;
     let us joyfully sing psalms to him.
R. *If today you hear his voice, harden not your hearts.*

[6] Come, let us bow down in worship;
     let us kneel before the LORD who made us.
[7ABC] For he is our God,
     and we are the people he shepherds, the
          flock he guides.
R. *If today you hear his voice, harden not your hearts.*

[7D] Oh, that today you would hear his voice:
     [8] "Harden not your hearts as at Meribah,
     as in the day of Massah in the desert,
[9] Where your fathers tempted me;
     they tested me though they had seen my

works."

R. If today you hear his voice, harden not your hearts.

Second Reading: 1 Corinthians 7:32-35

Brothers and sisters: ^{32}I should like you to be free of anxieties. An unmarried man is anxious about the things of the Lord, how he may please the Lord. ^{33}But a married man is anxious about the things of the world, how he may please his wife, ^{34}and he is divided. An unmarried woman or a virgin is anxious about the things of the Lord, so that she may be holy in both body and spirit. A married woman, on the other hand, is anxious about the things of the world, how she may please her husband. ^{5}I am telling you this for your own benefit, not to impose a restraint upon you, but for the sake of propriety and adherence to the Lord without distraction.

Alleluia: Matthew 4:16

R. Alleluia, alleluia.

^{16}The people who sit in darkness have seen a
        great light;
on those dwelling in a land overshadowed
        by death,
light has arisen.

R. Alleluia, alleluia.

Gospel: Mark 1:21-28

^{21}Then they came to Capernaum, and on the sabbath Jesus entered the synagogue and taught. ^{22}The people were astonished at his teaching, for he taught them as one having authority and not as the scribes. ^{23}In their synagogue was a man with an unclean spirit; ^{24}he cried out, "What have you to do with us, Jesus of Nazareth? Have you come to destroy us? I know who you are—the Holy One of God!" ^{25}Jesus rebuked him and said, "Quiet! Come out of him!" ^{26}The unclean spirit convulsed him and with a loud cry came out of him. ^{27}All were amazed and asked one another, "What is this? A new teaching with authority. He commands even the unclean spirits and they obey him." ^{28}His fame spread everywhere throughout the whole region of Galilee.

Sunday February 4, 2024

Fifth Sunday in Ordinary Time Year B
First Reading: Job 7:1-4, 6-7

Job spoke, saying:

¹ Is not man's life on earth a drudgery?
     Are not his days those of hirelings?
² He is a slave who longs for the shade,
     a hireling who waits for his wages.
³ So I have been assigned months of misery,
     and troubled nights have been allotted to
          me.
⁴ If in bed I say, "When shall I arise?"
     then the night drags on;
     I am filled with restlessness until the
          dawn.
⁶ My days are swifter than a weaver's shuttle;
     they come to an end without hope.
⁷ Remember that my life is like the wind;
     I shall not see happiness again.

Responsorial Psalm: Psalms 147:1-2,3-4, 5-6

R. *(cf. 3a)* **Praise the Lord, who heals the brokenhearted** *or:* **R. Alleluia.**
¹ Praise the LORD, for he is good;
     sing praise to our God, for he is gracious;
     it is fitting to praise him.
² The LORD rebuilds Jerusalem;
     the dispersed of Israel he gathers.
R. Praise the Lord, who heals the brokenhearted. *or:* **R. Alleluia.**
³ He heals the brokenhearted
     and binds up their wounds.
⁴ He tells the number of the stars;
     he calls each by name.
R. Praise the Lord, who heals the brokenhearted. *or:* **R. Alleluia.**

⁵ Great is our Lord and mighty in power;
     to his wisdom there is no limit.
⁶ The LORD sustains the lowly;
     the wicked he casts to the ground.
R. Praise the Lord, who heals the brokenhearted. *or:* **R. Alleluia.**

Second Reading: 1 Corinthians 9:16-19, 22-23

Brothers and sisters: ¹⁶ If I preach the gospel, this is no reason for me to boast, for an obligation has been imposed on me, and woe to me if I do not preach it! ¹⁷ If I do so willingly, I have a recompense, but if unwillingly, then I have been entrusted with a stewardship. ¹⁸ What then is my recompense? That, when I preach, I offer the gospel free of charge so as not to make full use of my right in the gospel.

¹⁹ Although I am free in regard to all, I have made myself a slave to all so as to win over as many as possible. ²² To the weak I became weak, to win over the weak. I have become all things to all, to save at least some. ²³ All this I do for the sake of the gospel, so that I too may have a share in it.

Alleluia: Matthew 8:17
R. Alleluia, alleluia.
¹⁷ Christ took away our infirmities
and bore our diseases.
R. Alleluia, alleluia.

Gospel: Mark 1:29-39
²⁹ On leaving the synagogue Jesus entered the house of Simon and Andrew with James and John. ³⁰ Simon's mother-in-law lay sick with a fever. They immediately told him about her. ³¹ He approached, grasped her hand, and helped her up. Then the fever left her and she waited on them.

³² When it was evening, after sunset, they brought to him all who were ill or possessed by demons. ³³ The whole town was gathered at the door. ³⁴ He cured many who were sick with various diseases, and he drove out many demons, not permitting them to speak because they knew him.

³⁵ Rising very early before dawn, he left and went off to a deserted place, where he prayed. ³⁶ Simon and those who were with him pursued him ³⁷ and on finding him said, "Everyone is looking for you." ³⁸ He told them, "Let us go on to the nearby villages that I may preach there also. For this purpose have I come." ³⁹ So he went into their synagogues, preaching and driving out demons throughout the whole of Galilee.

Sunday February 11, 2024

Sixth Sunday in ordinary Time Year B
First Reading: Leviticus 13:1-2, 44-46
¹ The LORD said to Moses and Aaron, ² "If someone has on his skin a scab or pustule or blotch which appears to be the sore of leprosy, he shall be brought to Aaron, the priest, or to one of the priests among his descendants. ⁴⁴ If the man is leprous and unclean, the priest shall declare him unclean by reason of the sore on his head.

⁴⁵ "The one who bears the sore of leprosy shall keep his garments rent and his head bare, and shall muffle his beard; he shall cry out, 'Unclean, unclean!' ⁴⁶ As

long as the sore is on him he shall declare himself unclean, since he is in fact unclean. He shall dwell apart, making his abode outside the camp."

Responsorial Psalm: Psalms 32:1-2, 5, 11
R. *(7) I turn to you, Lord, in time of trouble, and*
you fill me with the joy of salvation.
[1] Blessed is he whose fault is taken away,
whose sin is covered.
[2] Blessed the man to whom the LORD imputes
not guilt,
in whose spirit there is no guile.
R. *I turn to you, Lord, in time of trouble, and you*
fill me with the joy of salvation.
[5] Then I acknowledged my sin to you,
my guilt I covered not.
I said, "I confess my faults to the LORD,"
and you took away the guilt of my sin.
R. *I turn to you, Lord, in time of trouble, and you*
fill me with the joy of salvation.

[11] Be glad in the LORD and rejoice, you just;
exult, all you upright of heart.
R. *I turn to you, Lord, in time of trouble, and you*
fill me with the joy of salvation.

Second Reading: 1 Corinthians 10:31-11:1
Brothers and sisters, [31] Whether you eat or drink, or whatever you do, do everything for the glory of God. [32] Avoid giving offense, whether to the Jews or Greeks or the church of God, [33] just as I try to please everyone in every way, not seeking my own benefit but that of the many, that they may be saved. [1] Be imitators of me, as I am of Christ.

Alleluia: Luke 7:16
R. Alleluia, alleluia.
[16] A great prophet has arisen in our midst,
God has visited his people.
R. Alleluia, alleluia.

Gospel: Mark 1:40-45

[40] A leper came to Jesus and kneeling down begged him and said, "If you wish, you can make me clean." [41] Moved with pity, he stretched out his hand, touched him, and said to him, "I do will it. Be made clean." [42] The leprosy left him immediately, and he was made clean. [43] Then, warning him sternly, he dismissed him at once.

[44] He said to him, "See that you tell no one anything, but go, show yourself to the priest and offer for your cleansing what Moses prescribed; that will be proof for them."

[45] The man went away and began to publicize the whole matter. He spread the report abroad so that it was impossible for Jesus to enter a town openly. He remained outside in deserted places, and people kept coming to him from everywhere.

Sunday February 18, 2024

First Sunday of Lent, Year B
First Reading: Genesis 9:8-15

[8] God said to Noah and to his sons with him: [9] "See, I am now establishing my covenant with you and your descendants after you [10] and with every living creature that was with you: all the birds, and the various tame and wild animals that were with you and came out of the ark. [11] I will establish my covenant with you, that never again shall all bodily creatures be destroyed by the waters of a flood; there shall not be another flood to devastate the earth." [12] God added: "This is the sign that I am giving for all ages to come, of the covenant between me and you and every living creature with you: [13] I set my bow in the clouds to serve as a sign of the covenant between me and the earth. [14] When I bring clouds over the earth, and the bow appears in the clouds, [15] I will recall the covenant I have made between me and you and all living beings, so that the waters shall never again become a flood to destroy all mortal beings."

Responsorial Psalm: Psalms 25:4-5, 6-7, 8-9.
R. [(cf. 10)] *Your ways, O Lord, are love and truth to those who keep your covenant.*
[4] Your ways, O LORD, make known to me;
        teach me your paths.
[5] Guide me in your truth and teach me,
        for you are God my savior.
R. Your ways, O Lord, are love and truth to those who keep your covenant.

⁶ Remember that your compassion, O LORD,
    and your love are from of old.
⁷ In your kindness remember me,
    because of your goodness, O LORD.
R. *Your ways, O Lord, are love and truth to*
    those who keep your covenant.

⁸ Good and upright is the LORD,
    thus he shows sinners the way.
⁹ He guides the humble to justice,
    and he teaches the humble his way.
R. *Your ways, O Lord, are love and truth to*
    those who keep your covenant.

Second Reading: 1 Peter 3:18-22

Beloved: ¹⁸ Christ suffered for sins once, the righteous for the sake of the unrighteous, that he might lead you to God. Put to death in the flesh, he was brought to life in the Spirit. ¹⁹ In it he also went to preach to the spirits in prison, ²⁰ who had once been disobedient while God patiently waited in the days of Noah during the building of the ark, in which a few persons, eight in all, were saved through water. ²¹ This prefigured baptism, which saves you now. It is not a removal of dirt from the body but an appeal to God for a clear conscience, through the resurrection of Jesus Christ, ²² who has gone into heaven and is at the right hand of God, with angels, authorities, and powers subject to him.

Verse Before the Gospel: Matthew 4:4B

⁴ᴮ One does not live on bread alone,
but on every word that comes forth from the
    mouth of God.

Gospel: Mark 1:12-15

¹² The Spirit drove Jesus out into the desert, ¹³ and he remained in the desert for forty days, tempted by Satan. He was among wild beasts, and the angels ministered to him.

¹⁴ After John had been arrested, Jesus came to Galilee proclaiming the gospel of God: ¹⁵ "This is the time of fulfillment. The kingdom of God is at hand. Repent, and believe in the gospel."

Second Sunday of Lent, Year B
First Reading: Genesis 22:1-2, 9A, 10-13, 15-18

[1] God put Abraham to the test. He called to him, "Abraham!" "Here I am!" he replied. [2] Then God said: "Take your son Isaac, your only one, whom you love, and go to the land of Moriah. There you shall offer him up as a holocaust on a height that I will point out to you."

[9A] When they came to the place of which God had told him, Abraham built an altar there and arranged the wood on it. [10] Then he reached out and took the knife to slaughter his son. [11] But the LORD's messenger called to him from heaven, "Abraham, Abraham!" "Here I am!" he answered. [12] "Do not lay your hand on the boy," said the messenger. "Do not do the least thing to him. I know now how devoted you are to God, since you did not withhold from me your own beloved son." [13] As Abraham looked about, he spied a ram caught by its horns in the thicket. So he went and took the ram and offered it up as a holocaust in place of his son.

[15] Again the LORD's messenger called to Abraham from heaven [16] and said: "I swear by myself, declares the LORD, that because you acted as you did in not withholding from me your beloved son, [17] I will bless you abundantly and make your descendants as countless as the stars of the sky and the sands of the seashore; your descendants shall take possession of the gates of their enemies, [18] and in your descendants all the nations of the earth shall find blessing— all this because you obeyed my command."

Responsorial Psalm: Psalms 116:10, 15, 16-17, 18-19

R. [116:9] *I will walk before the Lord, in the land of the living.*

[10] I believed, even when I said,
"I am greatly afflicted."
[15] Precious in the eyes of the LORD
is the death of his faithful ones.

R. *I will walk before the Lord, in the land of the living.*

[16] O LORD, I am your servant;
I am your servant, the son of your handmaid;
you have loosed my bonds.
[17] To you will I offer sacrifice of thanksgiving,

and I will call upon the name of the LORD.
R. I will walk before the Lord, in the land of the
living.

¹⁸ My vows to the LORD I will pay
in the presence of all his people,
¹⁹ In the courts of the house of the LORD,
in your midst, O Jerusalem.
R. I will walk before the Lord, in the land of the
living.

Second Reading: Romans 8:31B-34

Brothers and sisters: ³¹ᴮ If God is for us, who can be against us? ³² He who did not spare his own Son but handed him over for us all, how will he not also give us everything else along with him?

³³ Who will bring a charge against God's chosen ones? It is God who acquits us. ³⁴ Who will condemn? Christ Jesus it is who died—or, rather, was raised—who also is at the right hand of God, who indeed intercedes for us.

Verse Before the Gospel: Matthew 17:5

⁵ From the shining cloud the Father's voice is
heard:
This is my beloved Son, listen to him.

Gospel: Mark 9:2-10

² Jesus took Peter, James, and John and led them up a high mountain apart by themselves. And he was transfigured before them, ³ and his clothes became dazzling white, such as no fuller on earth could bleach them. ⁴ Then Elijah appeared to them along with Moses, and they were conversing with Jesus. ⁵ Then Peter said to Jesus in reply, "Rabbi, it is good that we are here! Let us make three tents: one for you, one for Moses, and one for Elijah." ⁶ He hardly knew what to say, they were so terrified. ⁷ Then a cloud came, casting a shadow over them; from the cloud came a voice, "This is my beloved Son. Listen to him." ⁸ Suddenly, looking around, they no longer saw anyone but Jesus alone with them.

⁹ As they were coming down from the mountain, he charged them not to relate what they had seen to anyone, except when the Son of Man had risen from the dead. So they kept the matter to themselves, questioning what rising from the dead meant.

Third Sunday of Lent, Year B
First Reading: Exodus 20:1-17

[1] In those days, God delivered all these commandments: [2] "I, the LORD, am your God, who brought you out of the land of Egypt, that place of slavery. [3] You shall not have other gods besides me. [4] You shall not carve idols for yourselves in the shape of anything in the sky above or on the earth below or in the waters beneath the earth; [5] you shall not bow down before them or worship them. For I, the LORD, your God, am a jealous God, inflicting punishment for their fathers' wickedness on the children of those who hate me, down to the third and fourth generation; [6] but bestowing mercy down to the thousandth generation on the children of those who love me and keep my commandments.

[7] "You shall not take the name of the LORD, your God, in vain. For the LORD will not leave unpunished the one who takes his name in vain.

[8] "Remember to keep holy the sabbath day. [9] Six days you may labor and do all your work, [10] but the seventh day is the sabbath of the LORD, your God. No work may be done then either by you, or your son or daughter, or your male or female slave, or your beast, or by the alien who lives with you. [11] In six days the LORD made the heavens and the earth, the sea and all that is in them; but on the seventh day he rested. That is why the LORD has blessed the sabbath day and made it holy.

[12] "Honor your father and your mother, that you may have a long life in the land which the LORD, your God, is giving you. [13] You shall not kill. [14] You shall not commit adultery. [15] You shall not steal. [16] You shall not bear false witness against your neighbor. [17] You shall not covet your neighbor's house. You shall not covet your neighbor's wife, nor his male or female slave, nor his ox or ass, nor anything else that belongs to him."

Or Exodus 20:1-3, 7-8, 12-17

[1] In those days, God delivered all these commandments: [2] "I, the LORD, am your God, who brought you out of the land of Egypt, that place of slavery. [3] You shall not have other gods besides me.

[7] "You shall not take the name of the LORD, your God, in vain. For the LORD will not leave unpunished the one who takes his name in vain.

[8] "Remember to keep holy the sabbath day. [12] "Honor your father and your mother, that you may have a long life in the land which the LORD, your God, is giving you. [13] You shall not kill. [14] You shall not commit adultery. [15] You shall not steal. [16] You shall not bear false witness against your neighbor. [17] You shall not covet

your neighbor's house. You shall not covet your neighbor's wife, nor his male or female slave, nor his ox or ass, nor anything else that belongs to him."

Responsorial Psalm: Psalms 19:8, 9, 10, 11.

R. *(John 6:68c)* **Lord, you have the words of everlasting life.**

[8] The law of the LORD is perfect,
    refreshing the soul;
The decree of the LORD is trustworthy,
    giving wisdom to the simple.
R. Lord, you have the words of everlasting life.

[9] The precepts of the LORD are right,
    rejoicing the heart;
the command of the LORD is clear,
    enlightening the eye.
R. Lord, you have the words of everlasting life.

[10] The fear of the LORD is pure,
    enduring forever;
the ordinances of the LORD are true,
    all of them just.
R. Lord, you have the words of everlasting life.

[11] They are more precious than gold,
    than a heap of purest gold;
sweeter also than syrup
    or honey from the comb.
R. Lord, you have the words of everlasting life.

Second Reading: 1 Corinthians 1:22-25

Brothers and sisters: [22] Jews demand signs and Greeks look for wisdom, [23] but we proclaim Christ crucified, a stumbling block to Jews and foolishness to Gentiles, [24] but to those who are called, Jews and Greeks alike, Christ the power of God and the wisdom of God. [25] For the foolishness of God is wiser than human wisdom, and the weakness of God is stronger than human strength.

Verse Before the Gospel: John 3:16

[16] God so loved the world that he gave his only
    Son,

so that everyone who believes in him might
        have eternal life.

Gospel: John 2:13-25

¹³ Since the Passover of the Jews was near, Jesus went up to Jerusalem. ¹⁴ He found in the temple area those who sold oxen, sheep, and doves, as well as the money changers seated there. ¹⁵ He made a whip out of cords and drove them all out of the temple area, with the sheep and oxen, and spilled the coins of the money changers and overturned their tables, ¹⁶ and to those who sold doves he said, "Take these out of here, and stop making my Father's house a marketplace." ¹⁷ His disciples recalled the words of Scripture, *Zeal for your house will consume me*. ¹⁸ At this the Jews answered and said to him, "What sign can you show us for doing this?" ¹⁹ Jesus answered and said to them, "Destroy this temple and in three days I will raise it up." ²⁰ The Jews said, "This temple has been under construction for forty-six years, and you will raise it up in three days?" ²¹ But he was speaking about the temple of his body. ²² Therefore, when he was raised from the dead, his disciples remembered that he had said this, and they came to believe the Scripture and the word Jesus had spoken.

²³ While he was in Jerusalem for the feast of Passover, many began to believe in his name when they saw the signs he was doing. ²⁴ But Jesus would not trust himself to them because he knew them all, ²⁵ and did not need anyone to testify about
human nature. He himself understood it well.

Sunday March 10, 2024
Fourth Sunday of Lent, Year B
First Reading: 2 Chronicles 36:14-16, 19-23

¹⁴ In those days, all the princes of Judah, the priests, and the people added infidelity to infidelity, practicing all the abominations of the nations and polluting the LORD's temple which he had consecrated in Jerusalem.

¹⁵ Early and often did the LORD, the God of their fathers, send his messengers to them, for he had compassion on his people and his dwelling place. ¹⁶ But they mocked the messengers of God, despised his warnings, and scoffed at his prophets, until the anger of the LORD against his people was so inflamed that there was no remedy. ¹⁹ Their enemies burnt the house of God, tore down the walls of Jerusalem, set all its palaces afire, and destroyed all its precious objects. ²⁰ Those who escaped the sword were carried captive to Babylon, where they became servants of the king of the Chaldeans and his sons until the kingdom of the Persians came to power. ²¹ All this was to fulfill the word of the LORD spoken by

Jeremiah: "Until the land has retrieved its lost sabbaths, during all the time it lies waste it shall have rest while seventy years are fulfilled."

[22] In the first year of Cyrus, king of Persia, in order to fulfill the word of the LORD spoken by Jeremiah, the LORD inspired King Cyrus of Persia to issue this proclamation throughout his kingdom, both by word of mouth and in writing: [23] "Thus says Cyrus, king of Persia: All the kingdoms of the earth the LORD, the God of heaven, has given to me, and he has also charged me to build him a house in Jerusalem, which is in Judah. Whoever, therefore, among you belongs to any part of his people, let him go up, and may his God be with him!"

Responsorial Psalm: Psalms 137:1-2,3,4-5,6.

R. [6ab] *Let my tongue be silenced, if I ever forget you!*

[1] By the streams of Babylon
     we sat and wept when we remembered
        Zion.
[2] On the aspens of that land
     we hung up our harps.

R. *Let my tongue be silenced, if I ever forget you!*

[3] For there our captors asked of us
     the lyrics of our songs,
And our despoilers urged us to be joyous:
     "Sing for us the songs of Zion!"

R. *Let my tongue be silenced, if I ever forget you!*

[4] How could we sing a song of the LORD
     in a foreign land?
[5] If I forget you, Jerusalem,
     may my right hand be forgotten!

R. *Let my tongue be silenced, if I ever forget you!*

[6] May my tongue cleave to my palate
     if I remember you not,
If I place not Jerusalem
     ahead of my joy.

R. *Let my tongue be silenced, if I ever forget you!*

Second Reading: Ephesians 2:4-10

Brothers and sisters: [4] God, who is rich in mercy, because of the great love he had for us, [5] even when we were dead in our transgressions, brought us to life with

Christ— by grace you have been saved—, [6] raised us up with him, and seated us with him in the heavens in Christ Jesus, [7] that in the ages to come he might show the immeasurable riches of his grace in his kindness to us in Christ Jesus. [8] For by grace you have been saved through faith, and this is not from you; it is the gift of God; [9] it is not from works, so no one may boast. [10] For we are his handiwork, created in Christ Jesus for the good works that God has prepared in advance, that we should live in them.

Verse Before the Gospel: John 3:16

[16] God so loved the world that he gave his only
      Son,
so everyone who believes in him might have
      eternal life.

Gospel: John 3:14-21

Jesus said to Nicodemus: [14] "Just as Moses lifted up the serpent in the desert, so must the Son of Man be lifted up, [15] so that everyone who believes in him may have eternal life."

[16] For God so loved the world that he gave his only Son, so that everyone who believes in him might not perish but might have eternal life. [17] For God did not send his Son into the world to condemn the world, but that the world might be saved through him. [18] Whoever believes in him will not be condemned, but whoever does not believe has already been condemned, because he has not believed in the name of the only Son of God.

[19] And this is the verdict, that the light came into the world, but people preferred darkness to light, because their works were evil. [20] For everyone who does wicked things hates the light and does not come toward the light, so that his works might not be exposed. [21] But whoever lives the truth comes to the light, so that his works may be clearly seen as done in God.

Sunday March 17, 2024
Fifth Sunday of Lent, Year B

First Reading: Jeremiah 31:31-34

[31] The days are coming, says the LORD,
      when I will make a new covenant with
        the house of Israel
      and the house of Judah.
[32] It will not be like the covenant I made with
      their fathers
      the day I took them by the hand

to lead them forth from the land of Egypt;
    for they broke my covenant,
    and I had to show myself their master,
        says the LORD.
33 But this is the covenant that I will make
        with the house of Israel after those days,
        says the LORD.
I will place my law within them and write it
        upon their hearts;
    I will be their God, and they shall be my
        people.
34 No longer will they have need to teach their
        friends and relatives
    how to know the LORD.
All, from least to greatest, shall know me,
        says the LORD,
    for I will forgive their evildoing and
        remember their sin no more.

Responsorial Psalm: Psalms 51:3-4, 12-13, 14-15.
R. (12a) Create a clean heart in me, O God.
3 Have mercy on me, O God, in your goodness;
    in the greatness of your compassion wipe
        out my offense.
4 Thoroughly wash me from my guilt
    and of my sin cleanse me.
R. Create a clean heart in me, O God.

12 A clean heart create for me, O God,
    and a steadfast spirit renew within me.
13 Cast me not out from your presence,
    and your Holy Spirit take not from me.
R. Create a clean heart in me, O God.

14 Give me back the joy of your salvation,
    and a willing spirit sustain in me.
15 I will teach transgressors your ways,
    and sinners shall return to you.
R. Create a clean heart in me, O God.

Second Reading: Hebrews 5:7-9

7 In the days when Christ Jesus was in the flesh, he offered prayers and supplications with loud cries and tears to the one who was able to save him from death, and he was heard because of his reverence. 8 Son though he was, he learned obedience from what he suffered; 9 and when he was made perfect, he became the source of eternal salvation for all who obey him.

Verse Before the Gospel: John 12:26

26 Whoever serves me must follow me, says the
Lord;
and where I am, there also will my servant
be.

Gospel: John 12:20-33

20 Some Greeks who had come to worship at the Passover Feast 21 came to Philip, who was from Bethsaida in Galilee, and asked him, "Sir, we would like to see Jesus." 22 Philip went and told Andrew; then Andrew and Philip went and told Jesus. 23 Jesus answered them, "The hour has come for the Son of Man to be glorified. 24 Amen, amen, I say to you, unless a grain of wheat falls to the ground and dies, it remains just a grain of wheat; but if it dies, it produces much fruit. 25 Whoever loves his life loses it, and whoever hates his life in this world will preserve it for eternal life. 26 Whoever serves me must follow me, and where I am, there also will my servant be. The Father will honor whoever serves me.

27 "I am troubled now. Yet what should I say, 'Father, save me from this hour'? But it was for this purpose that I came to this hour. 28 Father, glorify your name." Then a voice came from heaven, "I have glorified it and will glorify it again." 29 The crowd there heard it and said it was thunder; but others said, "An angel has spoken to him." 30 Jesus answered and said, "This voice did not come for my sake but for yours. 31 Now is the time of judgment on this world; now the ruler of this world will be driven out. 32 And when I am lifted up from the earth, I will draw everyone to myself." He said this indicating the kind of death he would die.

Sunday March 24, 2024

Palm Sunday, Year B

At The Procession with Palms – Gospel – Mark 11: 1-10

1 When Jesus and his disciples drew near to Jerusalem, to Bethphage and Bethany at the Mount of Olives, he sent two of his disciples 2 and said to them, "Go into the village opposite you, and immediately on entering it, you will find a colt tethered on which no one has ever sat. Untie it and bring it here. 3 If anyone should say to you, 'Why are you doing this?' reply, 'The Master has need of it and will send it

back here at once.'" ⁴ So they went off and found a colt tethered at a gate outside on the street, and they untied it. ⁵ Some of the bystanders said to them, "What are you doing, untying the colt?" ⁶ They answered them just as Jesus had told them to, and they permitted them to do it. ⁷ So they brought the colt to Jesus and put their cloaks over it. And he sat on it. ⁸ Many people spread their cloaks on the road, and others spread leafy branches that they had cut from the fields. ⁹ Those preceding him as well as those following kept crying out:

"Hosanna!
    Blessed is he who comes in the name
        of the Lord!
    ¹⁰ Blessed is the kingdom of our father
        David that is to come!
Hosanna in the highest!"

Or John 12: 12-16
¹² When the great crowd that had come to the feast heard that Jesus was coming to Jerusalem, ¹³ they took palm branches and went out to meet him, and cried out:

"Hosanna!
Blessed is he who comes in the name of
        the Lord, the king of Israel."

¹⁴ Jesus found an ass and sat upon it, as is written:

¹⁵ *"Fear no more, O daughter Zion;*
see, your king comes, seated upon an
        ass's colt."

¹⁶ His disciples did not understand this at first, but when Jesus had been glorified they remembered that these things were written about him and that they had done this for him.

At The Mass – First Reading: Isaiah 50:4-7
⁴ The Lord GOD has given me
        a well-trained tongue,
that I might know how to speak to the weary
        a word that will rouse them.
Morning after morning

he opens my ear that I may hear;
⁵ and I have not rebelled,
    have not turned back.
        ⁶ I gave my back to those who beat me,
    my cheeks to those who plucked my
            beard;
my face I did not shield
    from buffets and spitting.

⁷ The Lord GOD is my help,
    therefore I am not disgraced;
I have set my face like flint,
    knowing that I shall not be put to shame.

Responsorial Psalm: Psalms 22:8-9, 17-18, 19-20, 23-24

R. *(2a) My God, my God, why have you
        abandoned me?*
⁸ All who see me scoff at me;
    they mock me with parted lips, they wag
        their heads:
⁹ "He relied on the LORD; let him deliver him,
    let him rescue him, if he loves him."
**R. My God, my God, why have you abandoned
        me?**

¹⁷ Indeed, many dogs surround me,
    a pack of evildoers closes in upon me;
¹⁸ They have pierced my hands and my feet;
    I can count all my bones.
**R. My God, my God, why have you abandoned
        me?**

¹⁹ They divide my garments among them,
    and for my vesture they cast lots.
²⁰ But you, O LORD, be not far from me;
    O my help, hasten to aid me.
**R. My God, my God, why have you abandoned
        me?**

²³ I will proclaim your name to my brethren;
      in the midst of the assembly I will praise
            you:
²⁴ "You who fear the LORD, praise him;
      all you descendants of Jacob, give glory to
            him;
      revere him, all you descendants of
            Israel!"
**R. My God, my God, why have you abandoned
            me?**

Second Reading: Philippians 2:6-11
⁶ Christ Jesus, though he was in the form of
            God,
      did not regard equality with God
      something to be grasped.
⁷ Rather, he emptied himself,
      taking the form of a slave,
      coming in human likeness;
      and found human in appearance,
      ⁸ he humbled himself,
      becoming obedient to the point of death,
      even death on a cross.
⁹ Because of this, God greatly exalted him
      and bestowed on him the name
      which is above every name,
      ¹⁰ that at the name of Jesus
      every knee should bend,
      of those in heaven and on earth and
            under the earth,
      ¹¹ and every tongue confess that
      Jesus Christ is Lord,
      to the glory of God the Father.

Verse Before the Gospel: Philippians 2:8-9
⁸ Christ became obedient to the point of death,
even death on a cross.
⁹ Because of this, God greatly exalted him
and bestowed on him the name which is

above every name.

Gospel: Mark 14: 1 – 15: 47

14:1 The Passover and the Feast of Unleavened Bread were to take place in two days' time. So the chief priests and the scribes were seeking a way to arrest him by treachery and put him to death. 2 They said, "Not during the festival, for fear that there may be a riot among the people."

3 When he was in Bethany reclining at table in the house of Simon the leper, a woman came with an alabaster jar of perfumed oil, costly genuine spikenard. She broke the alabaster jar and poured it on his head. 4 There were some who were indignant. "Why has there been this waste of perfumed oil? 5 It could have been sold for more than three hundred days' wages and the money given to the poor." They were infuriated with her. 6 Jesus said, "Let her alone. Why do you make trouble for her? She has done a good thing for me. 7 The poor you will always have with you, and whenever you wish you can do good to them, but you will not always have me. 8 She has done what she could. She has anticipated anointing my body for burial. 9 Amen, I say to you, wherever the gospel is proclaimed to the whole world, what she has done will be told in memory of her."

10 Then Judas Iscariot, one of the Twelve, went off to the chief priests to hand him over to them. 11 When they heard him they were pleased and promised to pay him money. Then he looked for an opportunity to hand him over.

12 On the first day of the Feast of Unleavened Bread, when they sacrificed the Passover lamb, his disciples said to him, "Where do you want us to go and prepare for you to eat the Passover?" 13 He sent two of his disciples and said to them, "Go into the city and a man will meet you, carrying a jar of water. Follow him. 14 Wherever he enters, say to the master of the house, 'The Teacher says, "Where is my guest room where I may eat the Passover with my disciples?"' 15 Then he will show you a large upper room furnished and ready. Make the preparations for us there." 16 The disciples then went off, entered the city, and found it just as he had told them; and they prepared the Passover.

17 When it was evening, he came with the Twelve. 18 And as they reclined at table and were eating, Jesus said, "Amen, I say to you, one of you will betray me, one who is eating with me." 19 They began to be distressed and to say to him, one by one, "Surely it is not I?" 20 He said to them, "One of the Twelve, the one who dips with me into the dish. 21 For the Son of Man indeed goes, as it is written of him, but woe to that man by whom the Son of Man is betrayed. It would be better for that man if he had never been born."

22 While they were eating, he took bread, said the blessing, broke it, and gave it to them, and said, "Take it; this is my body." 23 Then he took a cup, gave

thanks, and gave it to them, and they all drank from it. ²⁴ He said to them, "This is my blood of the covenant, which will be shed for many. ²⁵ Amen, I say to you, I shall not drink again the fruit of the vine until the day when I drink it new in the kingdom of God." ²⁶ Then, after singing a hymn, they went out to the Mount of Olives.

²⁷ Then Jesus said to them, "All of you will have your faith shaken, for it is written:

'I will strike the shepherd,
and the sheep will be dispersed.'

²⁸ But after I have been raised up, I shall go before you to Galilee." ²⁹ Peter said to him, "Even though all should have their faith shaken, mine will not be." ³⁰ Then Jesus said to him, "Amen, I say to you, this very night before the cock crows twice you will deny me three times." ³¹ But he vehemently replied, "Even though I should have to die with you, I will not deny you." And they all spoke similarly.

³² Then they came to a place named Gethsemane, and he said to his disciples, "Sit here while I pray." ³³ He took with him Peter, James, and John, and began to be troubled and distressed. ³⁴ Then he said to them, "My soul is sorrowful even to death. Remain here and keep watch." ³⁵ He advanced a little and fell to the ground and prayed that if it were possible the hour might pass by him; ³⁶ he said, "Abba, Father, all things are possible to you. Take this cup away from me, but not what I will but what you will." ³⁷ When he returned he found them asleep. He said to Peter, "Simon, are you asleep? Could you not keep watch for one hour? ³⁸ Watch and pray that you may not undergo the test. The spirit is willing but the flesh is weak." ³⁹ Withdrawing again, he prayed, saying the same thing. ⁴⁰ Then he returned once more and found them asleep, for they could not keep their eyes open and did not know what to answer him. ⁴¹ He returned a third time and said to them, "Are you still sleeping and taking your rest? It is enough. The hour has come. Behold, the Son of Man is to be handed over to sinners. ⁴² Get up, let us go. See, my betrayer is at hand."

⁴³ Then, while he was still speaking, Judas, one of the Twelve, arrived, accompanied by a crowd with swords and clubs who had come from the chief priests, the scribes, and the elders. ⁴⁴ His betrayer had arranged a signal with them, saying, "The man I shall kiss is the one; arrest him and lead him away securely." ⁴⁵ He came and immediately went over to him and said, "Rabbi." And he kissed him. ⁴⁶ At this they laid hands on him and arrested him. ⁴⁷ One of the bystanders drew his sword, struck the high priest's servant, and cut off his ear. ⁴⁸ Jesus said to them in reply, "Have you come out as against a robber, with swords and clubs, to seize me? ⁴⁹ Day after day I was with you teaching in the temple area, yet you did not

arrest me; but that the scriptures may be fulfilled." ⁵⁰ And they all left him and fled. ⁵¹ Now a young man followed him wearing nothing but a linen cloth about his body. They seized him, ⁵² but he left the cloth behind and ran off naked.

⁵³ They led Jesus away to the high priest, and all the chief priests and the elders and the scribes came together. ⁵⁴ Peter followed him at a distance into the high priest's courtyard and was seated with the guards, warming himself at the fire. ⁵⁵ The chief priests and the entire Sanhedrin kept trying to obtain testimony against Jesus in order to put him to death, but they found none. ⁵⁶ Many gave false witness against him, but their testimony did not agree. ⁵⁷ Some took the stand and testified falsely against him, alleging, ⁵⁸ "We heard him say, 'I will destroy this temple made with hands and within three days I will build another not made with hands.'" ⁵⁹ Even so their testimony did not agree. ⁶⁰ The high priest rose before the assembly and questioned Jesus, saying, "Have you no answer? What are these men testifying against you?" ⁶¹ But he was silent and answered nothing. Again the high priest asked him and said to him, "Are you the Messiah, the son of the Blessed One?" ⁶² Then Jesus answered, "I am;

and 'you will see the Son of Man
    seated at the right hand of the Power
    and coming with the clouds of
        heaven.'"

⁶³ At that the high priest tore his garments and said, "What further need have we of witnesses? ⁶⁴ You have heard the blasphemy. What do you think?" They all condemned him as deserving to die. ⁶⁵ Some began to spit on him. They blindfolded him and struck him and said to him, "Prophesy!" And the guards greeted him with blows.

⁶⁶ While Peter was below in the courtyard, one of the high priest's maids came along. ⁶⁷ Seeing Peter warming himself, she looked intently at him and said, "You too were with the Nazarene, Jesus." ⁶⁸ But he denied it saying, "I neither know nor understand what you are talking about." So he went out into the outer court. Then the cock crowed. ⁶⁹ The maid saw him and began again to say to the bystanders, "This man is one of them." ⁷⁰ Once again he denied it. A little later the bystanders said to Peter once more, "Surely you are one of them; for you too are a Galilean." ⁷¹ He began to curse and to swear, "I do not know this man about whom you are talking." ⁷² And immediately a cock crowed a second time. Then Peter remembered the word that Jesus had said to him, "Before the cock crows twice you will deny me three times." He broke down and wept.

¹⁵:¹ As soon as morning came, the chief priests with the elders and the scribes, that is, the whole Sanhedrin, held a council. They bound Jesus, led him

away, and handed him over to Pilate. ² Pilate questioned him, "Are you the king of the Jews?" He said to him in reply, "You say so." ³ The chief priests accused him of many things. ⁴ Again Pilate questioned him, "Have you no answer? See how many things they accuse you of." ⁵ Jesus gave him no further answer, so that Pilate was amazed.

⁶ Now on the occasion of the feast he used to release to them one prisoner whom they requested. ⁷ A man called Barabbas was then in prison along with the rebels who had committed murder in a rebellion. ⁸ The crowd came forward and began to ask him to do for them as he was accustomed. ⁹ Pilate answered, "Do you want me to release to you the king of the Jews?" ¹⁰ For he knew that it was out of envy that the chief priests had handed him over. ¹¹ But the chief priests stirred up the crowd to have him release Barabbas for them instead. ¹² Pilate again said to them in reply, "Then what do you want me to do with the man you call the king of the Jews?" ¹³ They shouted again, "Crucify him." ¹⁴ Pilate said to them, "Why? What evil has he done?" They only shouted the louder, "Crucify him." ¹⁵ So Pilate, wishing to satisfy the crowd, released Barabbas to them and, after he had Jesus scourged, handed him over to be crucified.

¹⁶ The soldiers led him away inside the palace, that is, the praetorium, and assembled the whole cohort. ¹⁷ They clothed him in purple and, weaving a crown of thorns, placed it on him. ¹⁸ They began to salute him with, "Hail, King of the Jews!" ¹⁹ and kept striking his head with a reed and spitting upon him. They knelt before him in homage. ²⁰ And when they had mocked him, they stripped him of the purple cloak, dressed him in his own clothes, and led him out to crucify him.

²¹ They pressed into service a passer-by, Simon, a Cyrenian, who was coming in from the country, the father of Alexander and Rufus, to carry his cross.

²² They brought him to the place of Golgotha—which is translated Place of the Skull—. ²³ They gave him wine drugged with myrrh, but he did not take it. ²⁴ Then they crucified him and divided his garments by casting lots for them to see what each should take. ²⁵ It was nine o'clock in the morning when they crucified him. ²⁶ The inscription of the charge against him read, "The King of the Jews." ²⁷ With him they crucified two revolutionaries, one on his right and one on his left. [28] ²⁹ Those passing by reviled him, shaking their heads and saying, "Aha! You who would destroy the temple and rebuild it in three days, ³⁰ save yourself by coming down from the cross." ³¹ Likewise the chief priests, with the scribes, mocked him among themselves and said, "He saved others; he cannot save himself. ³² Let the Christ, the King of Israel, come down now from the cross that we may see and believe." Those who were crucified with him also kept abusing him.

³³ At noon darkness came over the whole land until three in the afternoon. ³⁴ And at three o'clock Jesus cried out in a loud voice, "*Eloi, Eloi, lema sabachthani*?" which is translated, "My God, my God, why have you forsaken me?" ³⁵ Some of the

bystanders who heard it said, "Look, he is calling Elijah." ³⁶ One of them ran, soaked a sponge with wine, put it on a reed, and gave it to him to drink, saying, "Wait, let us see if Elijah comes to take him down." ³⁷ Jesus gave a loud cry and breathed his last.

(Here all kneel and pause for a short time)

³⁸ The veil of the sanctuary was torn in two from top to bottom. ³⁹ When the centurion who stood facing him saw how he breathed his last he said, "Truly this man was the Son of God!" ⁴⁰ There were also women looking on from a distance. Among them were Mary Magdalene, Mary the mother of the younger James and of Joses, and Salome. ⁴¹ These women had followed him when he was in Galilee and ministered to him. There were also many other women who had come up with him to Jerusalem.

⁴² When it was already evening, since it was the day of preparation, the day before the sabbath, ⁴³ Joseph of Arimathea, a distinguished member of the council, who was himself awaiting the kingdom of God, came and courageously went to Pilate and asked for the body of Jesus. ⁴⁴ Pilate was amazed that he was already dead. He summoned the centurion and asked him if Jesus had already died. ⁴⁵ And when he learned of it from the centurion, he gave the body to Joseph. ⁴⁶ Having bought a linen cloth, he took him down, wrapped him in the linen cloth and laid him in a tomb that had been hewn out of the rock. Then he rolled a stone against the entrance to the tomb. ⁴⁷ Mary Magdalene and Mary the mother of Joses watched where he was laid.

OR Mark 15:1-39

¹⁵:¹ As soon as morning came, the chief priests with the elders and the scribes, that is, the whole Sanhedrin, held a council. They bound Jesus, led him away, and handed him over to Pilate. ² Pilate questioned him, "Are you the king of the Jews?" He said to him in reply, "You say so." ³ The chief priests accused him of many things. ⁴ Again Pilate questioned him, "Have you no answer? See how many things they accuse you of." ⁵ Jesus gave him no further answer, so that Pilate was amazed.

⁶ Now on the occasion of the feast he used to release to them one prisoner whom they requested. ⁷ A man called Barabbas was then in prison along with the rebels who had committed murder in a rebellion. ⁸ The crowd came forward and began to ask him to do for them as he was accustomed. ⁹ Pilate answered, "Do you want me to release to you the king of the Jews?" ¹⁰ For he knew that it was out of envy that the chief priests had handed him over. ¹¹ But the chief priests stirred up the crowd to have him release Barabbas for them instead. ¹² Pilate again said to them in reply, "Then what do you want me to do with the man you call the king of the Jews?" ¹³ They shouted again, "Crucify him." ¹⁴ Pilate said to them, "Why?

What evil has he done?" They only shouted the louder, "Crucify him." ¹⁵ So Pilate, wishing to satisfy the crowd, released Barabbas to them and, after he had Jesus scourged, handed him over to be crucified.

¹⁶ The soldiers led him away inside the palace, that is, the praetorium, and assembled the whole cohort. ¹⁷ They clothed him in purple and, weaving a crown of thorns, placed it on him. ¹⁸ They began to salute him with, "Hail, King of the Jews!" ¹⁹ and kept striking his head with a reed and spitting upon him. They knelt before him in homage. ²⁰ And when they had mocked him, they stripped him of the purple cloak, dressed him in his own clothes, and led him out to crucify him.

²¹ They pressed into service a passer-by, Simon, a Cyrenian, who was coming in from the country, the father of Alexander and Rufus, to carry his cross.

²² They brought him to the place of Golgotha—which is translated Place of the Skull—. ²³ They gave him wine drugged with myrrh, but he did not take it. ²⁴ Then they crucified him and divided his garments by casting lots for them to see what each should take. ²⁵ It was nine o'clock in the morning when they crucified him. ²⁶ The inscription of the charge against him read, "The King of the Jews." ²⁷ With him they crucified two revolutionaries, one on his right and one on his left. [28] ²⁹ Those passing by reviled him, shaking their heads and saying, "Aha! You who would destroy the temple and rebuild it in three days, ³⁰ save yourself by coming down from the cross." ³¹ Likewise the chief priests, with the scribes, mocked him among themselves and said, "He saved others; he cannot save himself. ³² Let the Christ, the King of Israel, come down now from the cross that we may see and believe." Those who were crucified with him also kept abusing him.

³³ At noon darkness came over the whole land until three in the afternoon. ³⁴ And at three o'clock Jesus cried out in a loud voice, *"Eloi, Eloi, lema sabachthani*?" which is translated, "My God, my God, why have you forsaken me?" ³⁵ Some of the bystanders who heard it said, "Look, he is calling Elijah." ³⁶ One of them ran, soaked a sponge with wine, put it on a reed, and gave it to him to drink, saying, "Wait, let us see if Elijah comes to take him down." ³⁷ Jesus gave a loud cry and breathed his last.

(Here all kneel and pause for a short time)

³⁸ The veil of the sanctuary was torn in two from top to bottom. ³⁹ When the centurion who stood facing him saw how he breathed his last he said, "Truly this man was the Son of God!"

Sunday March 31, 2024
Easter Sunday

First Reading: Acts 10:34A, 37-43

^{34A} Peter proceeded to speak and said: ³⁷ "You know what has happened all over Judea, beginning in Galilee after the baptism that John preached, ³⁸ how God

anointed Jesus of Nazareth with the Holy Spirit and power. He went about doing good and healing all those oppressed by the devil, for God was with him. [39] We are witnesses of all that he did both in the country of the Jews and in Jerusalem. They put him to death by hanging him on a tree. [40] This man God raised on the third day and granted that he be visible, [41] not to all the people, but to us, the witnesses chosen by God in advance, who ate and drank with him after he rose from the dead. [42] He commissioned us to preach to the people and testify that he is the one appointed by God as judge of the living and the dead. [43] To him all the prophets bear witness, that everyone who believes in him will receive forgiveness of sins through his name."

Responsorial Psalm: Psalms 118:1-2, 16-17, 22-23.

R. [24] **This is the day the Lord has made; let us**
 rejoice and be glad. or: **R. Alleluia.**

[1] Give thanks to the LORD, for he is good,
 for his mercy endures forever.
[2] Let the house of Israel say,
 "His mercy endures forever."

R. This is the day the Lord has made; let us
 rejoice and be glad. or: **R. Alleluia.**

[16] The right hand of the LORD has struck with
 power;
 the right hand of the LORD is exalted.
[17] I shall not die, but live,
 and declare the works of the LORD.

R. This is the day the Lord has made; let us
 rejoice and be glad. or: **R. Alleluia.**

[22] The stone which the builders rejected
 has become the cornerstone.
[23] By the LORD has this been done;
 it is wonderful in our eyes.

R. This is the day the Lord has made; let us
 rejoice and be glad. or: **R. Alleluia.**

Second Reading: Colossians 3:1-4

Brothers and sisters: [1] If then you were raised with Christ, seek what is above, where Christ is seated at the right hand of God. [2] Think of what is above, not of what is on earth. [3] For you have died, and your life is hidden with Christ in God. [4] When Christ your life appears, then you too will appear with him in glory.

Or 1 Corinthians 5:6B-8

Brothers and sisters: [6B] Do you not know that a little yeast leavens all the dough? [7] Clear out the old yeast, so that you may become a fresh batch of dough, inasmuch as you are unleavened. For our paschal lamb, Christ, has been sacrificed. [8] Therefore, let us celebrate the feast, not with the old yeast, the yeast of malice and wickedness, but with the unleavened bread of sincerity and truth.

Sequence - *Victimae Paschali Laudes*

Christians, to the Paschal Victim
Offer your thankful praises!
A Lamb the sheep redeems;
Christ, who only is sinless,
Reconciles sinners to the Father.
Death and life have contended in that combat stupendous:
The Prince of life, who died, reigns immortal.
Speak, Mary, declaring
What you saw, wayfaring.
"The tomb of Christ, who is living,
The glory of Jesus' resurrection;
Bright angels attesting,
The shroud and napkin resting.
Yes, Christ my hope is arisen;
To Galilee he goes before you."
Christ indeed from death is risen, our new life obtaining.
Have mercy, victor King, ever reigning!
Amen. Alleluia.

Alleluia: cf. 1 Corinthians 5:7B-8A

R. Alleluia, alleluia.
[7B] Christ, our paschal lamb, has been
        sacrificed;
[8A] let us then feast with joy in the Lord.
R. Alleluia, alleluia.

Gospel: John 20:1-9

[1] On the first day of the week, Mary of Magdala came to the tomb early in the morning, while it was still dark, and saw the stone removed from the tomb. [2] So she ran and went to Simon Peter and to the other disciple whom Jesus loved, and told them, "They have taken the Lord from the tomb, and we don't know where they put him." [3] So Peter and the other disciple went out and came to the tomb. [4] They both ran, but the other disciple ran faster than Peter and arrived at the tomb first; [5] he bent down and saw the burial cloths there, but did not go in. [6] When Simon Peter arrived after him, he went into the tomb and saw the burial cloths there, [7] and the cloth that had covered his head, not with the burial cloths but rolled up in a separate place. [8] Then the other disciple also went in, the one who had arrived at the tomb first, and he saw and believed. [9] For they did not yet understand the Scripture that he had to rise from the dead.

Or Mark 16:1-7

[1] When the sabbath was over, Mary Magdalene, Mary, the mother of James, and Salome bought spices so that they might go and anoint him. [2] Very early when the sun had risen, on the first day of the week, they came to the tomb. [3] They were saying to one another, "Who will roll back the stone for us from the entrance to the tomb?" [4] When they looked up, they saw that the stone had been rolled back; it was very large. [5] On entering the tomb they saw a young man sitting on the right side, clothed in a white robe, and they were utterly amazed. [6] He said to them, "Do not be amazed! You seek Jesus of Nazareth, the crucified. He has been raised; he is not here. Behold the place where they laid him. [7] But go and tell his disciples and Peter, 'He is going before you to Galilee; there you will see him, as he told you.'"

Or Luke: 24:13-35

At an afternoon or evening Mass.

[13] That very day, the first day of the week, two of Jesus' disciples were going to a village seven miles from Jerusalem called Emmaus, [14] and they were conversing about all the things that had occurred. [15] And it happened that while they were conversing and debating, Jesus himself drew near and walked with them, [16] but their eyes were prevented from recognizing him. [17] He asked them, "What are you discussing as you walk along?" They stopped, looking downcast. [18] One of them, named Cleopas, said to him in reply, "Are you the only visitor to Jerusalem who does not know of the things that have taken place there in these days?" [19] And he replied to them, "What sort of things?" They said to him, "The things that happened to Jesus the Nazarene, who was a prophet mighty in deed and word before God and all the people, [20] how our chief priests and rulers both handed him over to a sentence of death and crucified him. [21] But we were hoping that he would

be the one to redeem Israel; and besides all this, it is now the third day since this took place. ²² Some women from our group, however, have astounded us: they were at the tomb early in the morning ²³ and did not find his body; they came back and reported that they had indeed seen a vision of angels who announced that he was alive. ²⁴ Then some of those with us went to the tomb and found things just as the women had described, but him they did not see." ²⁵ And he said to them, "Oh, how foolish you are! How slow of heart to believe all that the prophets spoke! ²⁶ Was it not necessary that the Christ should suffer these things and enter into his glory?" ²⁷ Then beginning with Moses and all the prophets, he interpreted to them what referred to him in all the Scriptures. ²⁸ As they approached the village to which they were going, he gave the impression that he was going on farther. ²⁹ But they urged him, "Stay with us, for it is nearly evening and the day is almost over." So he went in to stay with them. ³⁰ And it happened that, while he was with them at table, he took bread, said the blessing, broke it, and gave it to them. ³¹ With that their eyes were opened and they recognized him, but he vanished from their sight.

³² Then they said to each other, "Were not our hearts burning within us while he spoke to us on the way and opened the Scriptures to us?" ³³ So they set out at once and returned to Jerusalem where they found gathered together the eleven and those with them ³⁴ who were saying, "The Lord has truly been raised and has appeared to Simon!" ³⁵ Then the two recounted what had taken place on the way and how he was made known to them in the breaking of bread.

Sunday April 7, 2024

Second Sunday of Easter – Divine Mercy Sunday Year B
First Reading: Acts 4:32-35

³² The community of believers was of one heart and mind, and no one claimed that any of his possessions was his own, but they had everything in common. ³³ With great power the apostles bore witness to the resurrection of the Lord Jesus, and great favor was accorded them all. ³⁴ There was no needy person among them, for those who owned property or houses would sell them, bring the proceeds of the sale, ³⁵ and put them at the feet of the apostles, and they were distributed to each according to need.

Responsorial Psalm: Psalms 118:2-4, 13-15, 22-24
R. ⁽¹⁾ *Give thanks to the Lord for he is good,*
       his love is everlasting. or: *Alleluia.*
² Let the house of Israel say,
       "His mercy endures forever."
³ Let the house of Aaron say,
       "His mercy endures forever."

⁴ Let those who fear the LORD say,
"His mercy endures forever."

**R. Give thanks to the Lord for he is good, his
love is everlasting.** or: **Alleluia.**

¹³ I was hard pressed and was falling,
but the LORD helped me.

¹⁴ My strength and my courage is the LORD,
and he has been my savior.

¹⁵ The joyful shout of victory
in the tents of the just:

**R. Give thanks to the Lord for he is good, his
love is everlasting.** or: **Alleluia.**

²² The stone which the builders rejected
has become the cornerstone.

²³ By the LORD has this been done;
it is wonderful in our eyes.

²⁴ This is the day the LORD has made;
let us be glad and rejoice in it.

**R. Give thanks to the Lord for he is good, his
love is everlasting.** or: **Alleluia.**

Second Reading: 1 John 5:1-6

Beloved: ¹ Everyone who believes that Jesus is the Christ is begotten by God, and everyone who loves the Father loves also the one begotten by him. ² In this way we know that we love the children of God when we love God and obey his commandments. ³ For the love of God is this, that we keep his commandments. And his commandments are not burdensome, ⁴ for whoever is begotten by God conquers the world. And the victory that conquers the world is our faith. ⁵ Who indeed is the victor over the world but the one who believes that Jesus is the Son of God?

⁶ This is the one who came through water and blood, Jesus Christ, not by water alone, but by water and blood. The Spirit is the one that testifies, and the Spirit is truth.

Alleluia: John 20:29

R. Alleluia, alleluia.

²⁹ You believe in me, Thomas, because you
have seen me, says the Lord;

Blessed are those who have not seen me, but
　　　　still believe!
R. Alleluia, alleluia.

Gospel: John 20:19-31

[19] On the evening of that first day of the week, when the doors were locked, where the disciples were, for fear of the Jews, Jesus came and stood in their midst and said to them, "Peace be with you." [20] When he had said this, he showed them his hands and his side. The disciples rejoiced when they saw the Lord. [21] Jesus said to them again, "Peace be with you. As the Father has sent me, so I send you." [22] And when he had said this, he breathed on them and said to them, "Receive the Holy Spirit. [23] Whose sins you forgive are forgiven them, and whose sins you retain are retained."

[24] Thomas, called Didymus, one of the Twelve, was not with them when Jesus came. [25] So the other disciples said to him, "We have seen the Lord." But he said to them, "Unless I see the mark of the nails in his hands and put my finger into the nailmarks and put my hand into his side, I will not believe."

[26] Now a week later his disciples were again inside and Thomas was with them. Jesus came, although the doors were locked, and stood in their midst and said, "Peace be with you." [27] Then he said to Thomas, "Put your finger here and see my hands, and bring your hand and put it into my side, and do not be unbelieving, but believe." [28] Thomas answered and said to him, "My Lord and my God!" [29] Jesus said to him, "Have you come to believe because you have seen me? Blessed are those who have not seen and have believed."

[30] Now Jesus did many other signs in the presence of his disciples that are not written in this book. [31] But these are written that you may come to believe that Jesus is the Christ, the Son of God, and that through this belief you may have life in his name.

Sunday April 14, 2024

Third Sunday of Easter Year B
First Reading: Acts 3:13-15, 17-19

Peter said to the people: [13] "The God of Abraham, the God of Isaac, and the God of Jacob, the God of our fathers, has glorified his servant Jesus, whom you handed over and denied in Pilate's presence when he had decided to release him. [14] You denied the Holy and Righteous One and asked that a murderer be released to you. [15] The author of life you put to death, but God raised him from the dead; of this we are witnesses. [17] Now I know, brothers, that you acted out of ignorance, just as your leaders did; [18] but God has thus brought to fulfillment what he had announced beforehand through the mouth of all the prophets, that his Christ would suffer. [19] Repent, therefore, and be converted, that your sins may be wiped away."

Responsorial Psalm: Psalms 4:2, 4, 7-8, 9

R. [7a] **Lord, let your face shine on us.** or: **Alleluia.**

[2] When I call, answer me, O my just God,
> you who relieve me when I am in
> > distress;
> have pity on me, and hear my prayer!

R. Lord, let your face shine on us. or: **Alleluia.**

[4] Know that the LORD does wonders for his
> > faithful one;
> the LORD will hear me when I call upon him.

R. Lord, let your face shine on us. or: **Alleluia.**

[7] O LORD, let the light of your countenance
> > shine upon us!
> [8] You put gladness into my heart.

R. Lord, let your face shine on us. or: **Alleluia.**

[9] As soon as I lie down, I fall peacefully asleep,
> for you alone, O LORD,
> bring security to my dwelling.

R. Lord, let your face shine on us. or: **Alleluia.**

Second Reading: 1 John 2:1-5A

[1] My children, I am writing this to you so that you may not commit sin. But if anyone does sin, we have an Advocate with the Father, Jesus Christ the righteous one. [2] He is expiation for our sins, and not for our sins only but for those of the whole world. [3] The way we may be sure that we know him is to keep his commandments. [4] Those who say, "I know him," but do not keep his commandments are liars, and the truth is not in them. [5A] But whoever keeps his word, the love of God is truly perfected in him.

Alleluia: cf. Luke 24:32

R. Alleluia, alleluia.

[32] Lord Jesus, open the Scriptures to us;
make our hearts burn while you speak to us.

R. Alleluia, alleluia.

Gospel: Luke 24:35-48

[35] The two disciples recounted what had taken place on the way, and how Jesus was made known to them in the breaking of bread.

[36] While they were still speaking about this, he stood in their midst and said to them, "Peace be with you." [37] But they were startled and terrified and thought that they were seeing a ghost. [38] Then he said to them, "Why are you troubled? And why do questions arise in your hearts? [39] Look at my hands and my feet, that it is I myself. Touch me and see, because a ghost does not have flesh and bones as you can see I have." [40] And as he said this, he showed them his hands and his feet. [41] While they were still incredulous for joy and were amazed, he asked them, "Have you anything here to eat?" [42] They gave him a piece of baked fish; [43] he took it and ate it in front of them.

[44] He said to them, "These are my words that I spoke to you while I was still with you, that everything written about me in the law of Moses and in the prophets and psalms must be fulfilled." [45] Then he opened their minds to understand the Scriptures. [46] And he said to them, "Thus it is written that the Christ would suffer and rise from the dead on the third day [47] and that repentance, for the forgiveness of sins, would be preached in his name to all the nations, beginning from Jerusalem. [48] You are witnesses of these things."

Sunday April 21, 2024

Fourth Sunday of Easter, Year B
First Reading: Acts 4:8-12

[8] Peter, filled with the Holy Spirit, said: "Leaders of the people and elders: [9] If we are being examined today about a good deed done to a cripple, namely, by what means he was saved, [10] then all of you and all the people of Israel should know that it was in the name of Jesus Christ the Nazorean whom you crucified, whom God raised from the dead; in his name this man stands before you healed. [11] *He is the stone rejected by you, the builders, which has become the cornerstone.* [12] There is no salvation through anyone else, nor is there any other name under heaven given to the human race by which we are to be saved."

Responsorial Psalm: Psalms 118:1, 8-9, 21-23, 26, 28, 29

R. [22] *The stone rejected by the builders has become the cornerstone.* or: *Alleluia.*

[1] Give thanks to the LORD, for he is good,
      for his mercy endures forever.
[8] It is better to take refuge in the LORD

      than to trust in man.

⁹ It is better to take refuge in the LORD
      than to trust in princes.

R. The stone rejected by the builders has become the cornerstone. or: **Alleluia.**

²¹ I will give thanks to you, for you have
      answered me
    and have been my savior.

²² The stone which the builders rejected
      has become the cornerstone.

²³ By the LORD has this been done;
      it is wonderful in our eyes.

R. The stone rejected by the builders has become the cornerstone. or: **Alleluia.**

²⁶ Blessed is he who comes in the name of the
      LORD;
    we bless you from the house of the LORD.

²⁸ I will give thanks to you, for you have
      answered me
    and have been my savior.

²⁹ Give thanks to the LORD, for he is good;
      for his kindness endures forever.

R. The stone rejected by the builders has become the cornerstone. or: **Alleluia.**

Second Reading: 1 John 3:1-2

Beloved: ¹ See what love the Father has bestowed on us that we may be called the children of God. Yet so we are. The reason the world does not know us is that it did not know him. ² Beloved, we are God's children now; what we shall be has not yet been revealed. We do know that when it is revealed we shall be like him, for we shall see him as he is.

Alleluia: John 10:14

R. Alleluia, alleluia.

¹⁴ I am the good shepherd, says the Lord;
I know my sheep, and mine know me.

R. Alleluia, alleluia.

Gospel: John 10:11-18

Jesus said: [11] "I am the good shepherd. A good shepherd lays down his life for the sheep. [12] A hired man, who is not a shepherd and whose sheep are not his own, sees a wolf coming and leaves the sheep and runs away, and the wolf catches and scatters them. [13] This is because he works for pay and has no concern for the sheep. [14] I am the good shepherd, and I know mine and mine know me, [15] just as the Father knows me and I know the Father; and I will lay down my life for the sheep. [16] I have other sheep that do not belong to this fold. These also I must lead, and they will hear my voice, and there will be one flock, one shepherd. [17] This is why the Father loves me, because I lay down my life in order to take it up again. [18] No one takes it from me, but I lay it down on my own. I have power to lay it down, and power to take it up again. This command I have received from my Father."

Sunday April 28, 2024
Fifth Sunday of Easter, Year B

First Reading: Acts 9:26-31

[26] When Saul arrived in Jerusalem he tried to join the disciples, but they were all afraid of him, not believing that he was a disciple. [27] Then Barnabas took charge of him and brought him to the apostles, and he reported to them how he had seen the Lord, and that he had spoken to him, and how in Damascus he had spoken out boldly in the name of Jesus. [28] He moved about freely with them in Jerusalem, and spoke out boldly in the name of the Lord. [29] He also spoke and debated with the Hellenists, but they tried to kill him. [30] And when the brothers learned of this, they took him down to Caesarea and sent him on his way to Tarsus.

[31] The church throughout all Judea, Galilee, and Samaria was at peace. It was being built up and walked in the fear of the Lord, and with the consolation of the Holy Spirit it grew in numbers.

Responsorial Psalm: Psalms 22:26-27, 28, 30, 31-32

R. [26a] *I will praise you, Lord, in the assembly of*
your people. or: *Alleluia.*

[26] I will fulfill my vows before those who fear
the LORD.
[27] The lowly shall eat their fill;
they who seek the LORD shall praise him:
"May your hearts live forever!"

R. *I will praise you, Lord, in the assembly of your*
people. or: *Alleluia.*

²⁸ All the ends of the earth
        shall remember and turn to the LORD;
all the families of the nations
        shall bow down before him.
**R. I will praise you, Lord, in the assembly of your
                people. or: Alleluia.**

³⁰ To him alone shall bow down
        all who sleep in the earth;
before him shall bend
        all who go down into the dust.
**R. I will praise you, Lord, in the assembly of your
                people. or: Alleluia.**

³¹ And to him my soul shall live;
        my descendants shall serve him.
³² Let the coming generation be told of the LORD
        that they may proclaim to a people yet to
                be born
        the justice he has shown.
**R. I will praise you, Lord, in the assembly of your
                people. or: Alleluia.**

Second Reading: 1 John 3:18-24

¹⁸ Children, let us love not in word or speech but in deed and truth. ¹⁹ Now this is how we shall know that we belong to the truth and reassure our hearts before him ²⁰ in whatever our hearts condemn, for God is greater than our hearts and knows everything. ²¹ Beloved, if our hearts do not condemn us, we have confidence in God ²² and receive from him whatever we ask, because we keep his commandments and do what pleases him. ²³ And his commandment is this: we should believe in the name of his Son, Jesus Christ, and love one another just as he commanded us. ²⁴ Those who keep his commandments remain in him, and he in them, and the way we know that he remains in us is from the Spirit he gave us.

Alleluia: John 15:4A, 5B
R. Alleluia, alleluia.
⁴ᴬ Remain in me as I remain in you, says the
                Lord.
⁵ᴮ Whoever remains in me will bear much

fruit.
R. Alleluia, alleluia.

Gospel: John 15:1-8

Jesus said to his disciples: [1] "I am the true vine, and my Father is the vine grower. [2] He takes away every branch in me that does not bear fruit, and every one that does he prunes so that it bears more fruit. [3] You are already pruned because of the word that I spoke to you. [4] Remain in me, as I remain in you. Just as a branch cannot bear fruit on its own unless it remains on the vine, so neither can you unless you remain in me. [5] I am the vine, you are the branches. Whoever remains in me and I in him will bear much fruit, because without me you can do nothing. [6] Anyone who does not remain in me will be thrown out like a branch and wither; people will gather them and throw them into a fire and they will be burned. [7] If you remain in me and my words remain in you, ask for whatever you want and it will be done for you. [8] By this is my Father glorified, that you bear much fruit and become my disciples."

Sunday May 5, 2024
Sixth Sunday of Easter, Year B

First Reading: Acts 10:25-26, 34-35, 44-48

[25] When Peter entered, Cornelius met him and, falling at his feet, paid him homage. [26] Peter, however, raised him up, saying, "Get up. I myself am also a human being."

[34] Then Peter proceeded to speak and said, "In truth, I see that God shows no partiality. [35] Rather, in every nation whoever fears him and acts uprightly is acceptable to him."

[44] While Peter was still speaking these things, the Holy Spirit fell upon all who were listening to the word. [45] The circumcised believers who had accompanied Peter were astounded that the gift of the Holy Spirit should have been poured out on the Gentiles also, [46] for they could hear them speaking in tongues and glorifying God. Then Peter responded, [47] "Can anyone withhold the water for baptizing these people, who have received the Holy Spirit even as we have?" [48] He ordered them to be baptized in the name of Jesus Christ.

Responsorial Psalm: Psalms 98:1, 2-3, 3-4

R. *(cf. 2b)* ***The Lord has revealed to the nations his
saving power.*** or: ***Alleluia.***

[1] Sing to the LORD a new song,
for he has done wondrous deeds;

His right hand has won victory for him,
    his holy arm.
**R. The Lord has revealed to the nations his
    saving power.** or: **Alleluia.**

[2] The LORD has made his salvation known:
    in the sight of the nations he has revealed
        his justice.
[3AB] He has remembered his kindness and his
    faithfulness
    toward the house of Israel.
**R. The Lord has revealed to the nations his
    saving power.** or: **Alleluia.**

[3BC] All the ends of the earth have seen
    the salvation by our God.
[4] Sing joyfully to the LORD, all you lands;
    break into song; sing praise.
**R. The Lord has revealed to the nations his
    saving power.** or: **Alleluia.**

Second Reading: 1 John 4:7-10

[7] Beloved, let us love one another, because love is of God; everyone who loves is begotten by God and knows God. [8] Whoever is without love does not know God, for God is love. [9] In this way the love of God was revealed to us: God sent his only Son into the world so that we might have life through him. [10] In this is love: not that we have loved God, but that he loved us and sent his Son as expiation for our sins.

Alleluia: John 14:23

R. Alleluia, alleluia.
[23] Whoever loves me will keep my word,
    says the Lord,
and my Father will love him and we will
    come to him.
R. Alleluia, alleluia.

Gospel: John 15:9-17

Jesus said to his disciples: [9] "As the Father loves me, so I also love you. Remain in my love. [10] If you keep my commandments, you will remain in my love, just as I have kept my Father's commandments and remain in his love.

[11] "I have told you this so that my joy may be in you and your joy might be complete. [12] This is my commandment: love one another as I love you. [13] No one has greater love than this, to lay down one's life for one's friends. [14] You are my friends if you do what I command you. [15] I no longer call you slaves, because a slave does not know what his master is doing. I have called you friends, because I have told you everything I have heard from my Father. [16] It was not you who chose me, but I who chose you and appointed you to go and bear fruit that will remain, so that whatever you ask the Father in my name he may give you. [17] This I command you: love one another."

Sunday May 12, 2024
Solemnity of Ascension of the Lord

First Reading: Acts 1:1-11

[1] In the first book, Theophilus, I dealt with all that Jesus did and taught [2] until the day he was taken up, after giving instructions through the Holy Spirit to the apostles whom he had chosen. [3] He presented himself alive to them by many proofs after he had suffered, appearing to them during forty days and speaking about the kingdom of God. [4] While meeting with them, he enjoined them not to depart from Jerusalem, but to wait for "the promise of the Father about which you have heard me speak; [5] for John baptized with water, but in a few days you will be baptized with the Holy Spirit."

[6] When they had gathered together they asked him, "Lord, are you at this time going to restore the kingdom to Israel?" [7] He answered them, "It is not for you to know the times or seasons that the Father has established by his own authority. [8] But you will receive power when the Holy Spirit comes upon you, and you will be my witnesses in Jerusalem, throughout Judea and Samaria, and to the ends of the earth." [9] When he had said this, as they were looking on, he was lifted up, and a cloud took him from their sight. [10] While they were looking intently at the sky as he was going, suddenly two men dressed in white garments stood beside them. [11] They said, "Men of Galilee, why are you standing there looking at the sky? This Jesus who has been taken up from you into heaven will return in the same way as you have seen him going into heaven."

Responsorial Psalm: Psalms 47:2-3, 6-7, 8-9
R. [(6)] *God mounts his throne to shouts of joy: a*
blare of trumpets for the Lord.
or: *Alleluia.*
[2] All you peoples, clap your hands,

shout to God with cries of gladness,
³ For the LORD, the Most High, the awesome,
    is the great king over all the earth.
R. God mounts his throne to shouts of joy: a
         blare of trumpets for the Lord.
or: **Alleluia.**

⁶ God mounts his throne amid shouts of joy;
    the LORD, amid trumpet blasts.
⁷ Sing praise to God, sing praise;
    sing praise to our king, sing praise.
R. God mounts his throne to shouts of joy: a
         blare of trumpets for the Lord.
or: **Alleluia.**

⁸ For king of all the earth is God;
    sing hymns of praise.
⁹ God reigns over the nations,
    God sits upon his holy throne.
R. God mounts his throne to shouts of joy: a
         blare of trumpets for the Lord.
or: **Alleluia.**

Second Reading: Ephesians 1:17-23

Brothers and sisters: ¹⁷ May the God of our Lord Jesus Christ, the Father of glory, give you a Spirit of wisdom and revelation resulting in knowledge of him. ¹⁸ May the eyes of your hearts be enlightened, that you may know what is the hope that belongs to his call, what are the riches of glory in his inheritance among the holy ones,¹⁹ and what is the surpassing greatness of his power for us who believe, in accord with the exercise of his great might, ²⁰ which he worked in Christ, raising him from the dead and seating him at his right hand in the heavens, ²¹ far above every principality, authority, power, and dominion, and every name that is named not only in this age but also in the one to come. ²² And he put all things beneath his feet and gave him as head over all things to the church, which is his body, the fullness of the one who fills all things in every way.

OR Ephesians 4:1-13

¹ Brothers and sisters, I, a prisoner for the Lord, urge you to live in a manner worthy of the call you have received, ² with all humility and gentleness, with patience,

bearing with one another through love, [3] striving to preserve the unity of the Spirit through the bond of peace: [4] one body and one Spirit, as you were also called to the one hope of your call; [5] one Lord, one faith, one baptism; [6] one God and Father of all, who is over all and through all and in all.

[7] But grace was given to each of us according to the measure of Christ's gift. [8] Therefore, it says: *He ascended on high and took prisoners captive; he gave gifts to men*. [9] What does "he ascended" mean except that he also descended into the lower regions of the earth? [10] The one who descended is also the one who ascended far above all the heavens, that he might fill all things.

[11] And he gave some as apostles, others as prophets, others as evangelists, others as pastors and teachers,[12] to equip the holy ones for the work of ministry, for building up the body of Christ, [13] until we all attain to the unity of faith and knowledge of the Son of God, to mature manhood, to the extent of the full stature of Christ.

OR Ephesians 4:1-7, 11-13

[1] Brothers and sisters, I, a prisoner for the Lord, urge you to live in a manner worthy of the calling you have received, [2] with all humility and gentleness, with patience, bearing with one another through love, [3] striving to preserve the unity of the Spirit through the bond of peace: [4] one body and one Spirit, as you were also called to the one hope of your calling; [5] one Lord, one faith, one baptism; [6] one God and Father of all, who is over all and through all and in all.

[7] But grace was given to each of us according to the measure of Christ's gift.

[11] And he gave some as apostles, others as prophets, others as evangelists, others as pastors and teachers, [12] to equip the holy ones for the work of ministry, for building up the body of Christ, [13] until we all attain to the unity of faith and knowledge of the Son of God, to mature manhood, to the extent of the full stature of Christ.

Alleluia: Matthew 28:19A, 20B
R. Alleluia, alleluia.
[19A] Go and teach all nations, says the Lord;
[20B] I am with you always, until the end of the
world.
R. Alleluia, alleluia.

Gospel: Mark 16: 15-20
[15] Jesus said to his disciples: "Go into the whole world and proclaim the gospel to every creature. [16] Whoever believes and is baptized will be saved; whoever does not believe will be condemned. [17] These signs will accompany those who believe: in my name they will drive out demons, they will speak new languages. [18] They will pick up serpents with

their hands, and if they drink any deadly thing, it will not harm them. They will lay hands on the sick, and they will recover."

[19] So then the Lord Jesus, after he spoke to them, was taken up into heaven and took his seat at the right hand of God. [20] But they went forth and preached everywhere, while the Lord worked with them and confirmed the word through accompanying signs.

Sunday May 19, 2024
Pentecost Sunday

First Reading: Acts 2:1-11

[1] When the time for Pentecost was fulfilled, they were all in one place together. [2] And suddenly there came from the sky a noise like a strong driving wind, and it filled the entire house in which they were. [3] Then there appeared to them tongues as of fire, which parted and came to rest on each one of them. [4] And they were all filled with the Holy Spirit and began to speak in different tongues, as the Spirit enabled them to proclaim.

[5] Now there were devout Jews from every nation under heaven staying in Jerusalem. [6] At this sound, they gathered in a large crowd, but they were confused because each one heard them speaking in his own language. [7] They were astounded, and in amazement, they asked, "Are not all these people who are speaking Galileans? [8] Then how does each of us hear them in his native language? [9] We are Parthians, Medes, and Elamites, inhabitants of Mesopotamia, Judea and Cappadocia, Pontus and Asia, [10] Phrygia and Pamphylia, Egypt and the districts of Libya near Cyrene, as well as travellers from Rome, [11] both Jews and converts to Judaism, Cretans and Arabs, yet we hear them speaking in our own tongues of the mighty acts of God."

Responsorial Psalm: Psalms 104:1, 24, 29-30, 31, 34

R. (cf. 30) *Lord, send out your Spirit, and renew the face of the earth.* or: *Alleluia.*

[1] Bless the LORD, O my soul!
O LORD, my God, you are great indeed!
[24] How manifold are your works, O LORD!
The earth is full of your creatures;

R. *Lord, send out your Spirit, and renew the face of the earth.* or: *Alleluia.*

[29] If you take away their breath, they perish
and return to their dust.

[30] When you send forth your spirit, they are
created,
and you renew the face of the earth.
**R. Lord, send out your Spirit, and renew the face
of the earth.** or: *Alleluia.*

[31] May the glory of the LORD endure forever;
may the LORD be glad in his works!
[34] Pleasing to him be my theme;
I will be glad in the LORD.
**R. Lord, send out your Spirit, and renew the face
of the earth.** or: *Alleluia.*

Second Reading: 1 Corinthians 12:3B-7, 12-13

Brothers and sisters: [3B] No one can say, "Jesus is Lord," except by the Holy Spirit. [4] There are different kinds of spiritual gifts but the same Spirit; [5] there are different forms of service but the same Lord; [6] there are different workings but the same God who produces all of them in everyone. [7] To each individual the manifestation of the Spirit is given for some benefit.

[12] As a body is one though it has many parts, and all the parts of the body, though many, are one body, so also Christ. [13] For in one Spirit we were all baptized into one body, whether Jews or Greeks, slaves or free persons, and we were all given to drink of one Spirit.

OR Galatians 5:16-25

[16] Brothers and sisters, live by the Spirit and you will certainly not gratify the desire of the flesh. [17] For the flesh has desires against the Spirit, and the Spirit against the flesh; these are opposed to each other, so that you may not do what you want. [18] But if you are guided by the Spirit, you are not under the law. [19] Now the works of the flesh are obvious: immorality, impurity, lust, [20] idolatry, sorcery, hatreds, rivalry, jealousy, outbursts of fury, acts of selfishness, dissensions, factions, [21] occasions of envy, drinking bouts, orgies, and the like. I warn you, as I warned you before, that those who do such things will not inherit the kingdom of God. [22] In contrast, the fruit of the Spirit is love, joy, peace, patience, kindness, generosity, faithfulness, [23] gentleness, self-control. Against such there is no law. [24] Now those who belong to Christ Jesus have crucified their flesh with its passions and desires. [25] If we live in the Spirit, let us also follow the Spirit.

Sequence - *Veni, Sancte Spiritus*

Come, Holy Spirit, come!
And from your celestial home
Shed a ray of light divine!
Come, Father of the poor!
Come, source of all our store!
Come, within our bosoms shine.
You, of comforters the best;
You, the soul's most welcome guest;
Sweet refreshment here below;
In our labor, rest most sweet;
Grateful coolness in the heat;
Solace in the midst of woe.
O most blessed Light divine,
Shine within these hearts of yours,
And our inmost being fill!
Where you are not, we have naught,
Nothing good in deed or thought,
Nothing free from taint of ill.
Heal our wounds, our strength renew;
On our dryness pour your dew;
Wash the stains of guilt away:
Bend the stubborn heart and will;
Melt the frozen, warm the chill;
Guide the steps that go astray.
On the faithful, who adore
And confess you, evermore
In your sevenfold gift descend;
Give them virtue's sure reward;
Give them your salvation, Lord;
Give them joys that never end. Amen.
Alleluia.

Alleluia
R. Alleluia, alleluia.
Come, Holy Spirit, fill the hearts of your
          faithful
and kindle in them the fire of your love.
R. Alleluia, alleluia.

Gospel: John 20:19-23

¹⁹ On the evening of that first day of the week, when the doors were locked, where the disciples were, for fear of the Jews, Jesus came and stood in their midst and said to them, "Peace be with you." ²⁰ When he had said this, he showed them his hands and his side. The disciples rejoiced when they saw the Lord. ²¹ Jesus said to them again, "Peace be with you. As the Father has sent me, so I send you." ²² And when he had said this, he breathed on them and said to them, "Receive the Holy Spirit. ²³ Whose sins you forgive are forgiven them, and whose sins you retain are retained."

Or: John 15:26-27; 16:12-15

Jesus said to his disciples: ²⁶ "When the Advocate comes whom I will send you from the Father, the Spirit of truth that proceeds from the Father, he will testify to me. ²⁷ And you also testify, because you have been with me from the beginning.

¹² "I have much more to tell you, but you cannot bear it now. ¹³ But when he comes, the Spirit of truth, he will guide you to all truth. He will not speak on his own, but he will speak what he hears, and will declare to you the things that are coming. ¹⁴ He will glorify me, because he will take from what is mine and declare it to you. ¹⁵ Everything that the Father has is mine; for this reason I told you that he will take from what is mine and declare it to you."

Sunday May 26, 2024
Solemnity of the Most Holy Trinity
First Reading: Deuteronomy 4:32-34, 39-40

³² Moses said to the people: "Ask now of the days of old, before your time, ever since God created man upon the earth; ask from one end of the sky to the other: Did anything so great ever happen before? Was it ever heard of? ³³ Did a people ever hear the voice of God speaking from the midst of fire, as you did, and live? ³⁴ Or did any god venture to go and take a nation for himself from the midst of another nation, by testings, by signs and wonders, by war, with strong hand and outstretched arm, and by great terrors, all of which the LORD, your God, did for you in Egypt before your very eyes? ³⁹ This is why you must now know, and fix in your heart, that the LORD is God in the heavens above and on earth below, and that there is no other. ⁴⁰ You must keep his statutes and commandments that I enjoin on you today, that you and your children after you may prosper, and that you may have long life on the land which the LORD, your God, is giving you forever."

Responsorial Psalm: Psalms 33:4-5, 6, 9, 18-19, 20, 22
R. *(12b)* **Blessed the people the Lord has chosen**

to be his own.

[4] Upright is the word of the LORD,
    and all his works are trustworthy.
[5] He loves justice and right;
    of the kindness of the LORD the earth is
        full.

*R. Blessed the people the Lord has chosen to be
        his own.*

[6] By the word of the LORD the heavens were
        made;
    by the breath of his mouth all their host.
[9] For he spoke, and it was made;
    he commanded, and it stood forth.

*R. Blessed the people the Lord has chosen to be
        his own.*

[18] See, the eyes of the LORD are upon those who
        fear him,
    upon those who hope for his kindness,
[19] to deliver them from death
    and preserve them in spite of famine.

*R. Blessed the people the Lord has chosen to be
        his own.*

[20] Our soul waits for the LORD,
    who is our help and our shield.
[22] May your kindness, O LORD, be upon us
    who have put our hope in you.

*R. Blessed the people the Lord has chosen to be
        his own.*

Second Reading: Romans 8:14-17

Brothers and sisters: [14] Those who are led by the Spirit of God are sons of God. [15] For you did not receive a spirit of slavery to fall back into fear, but you received a Spirit of adoption, through whom we cry, "Abba, Father!" [16] The Spirit himself bears witness with our spirit that we are children of God, [17]and if children, then heirs, heirs of God and joint heirs with Christ, if only we suffer with him so that we may also be glorified with him.

Alleluia: Revelation 1:8

R. Alleluia, alleluia.

[8] Glory to the Father, the Son, and the Holy
    Spirit;
to God who is, who was, and who is to come.

R. Alleluia, alleluia.

Gospel: Matthew 28:16-20

[16] The eleven disciples went to Galilee, to the mountain to which Jesus had ordered them. [17] When they all saw him, they worshiped, but they doubted. [18] Then Jesus approached and said to them, "All power in heaven and on earth has been given to me. [19] Go, therefore, and make disciples of all nations, baptizing them in the name of the Father, and of the Son, and of the Holy Spirit, [20] teaching them to observe all that I have commanded you. And behold, I am with you always, until the end of the age."

Sunday June 2, 2024

Solemnity of Body and Blood of Christ (*Corpus Christi*)

First Reading: Exodus 24:3-8

[3] When Moses came to the people and related all the words and ordinances of the LORD, they all answered with one voice, "We will do everything that the LORD has told us." [4] Moses then wrote down all the words of the LORD and, rising early the next day, he erected at the foot of the mountain an altar and twelve pillars for the twelve tribes of Israel. [5] Then, having sent certain young men of the Israelites to offer holocausts and sacrifice young bulls as peace offerings to the LORD, [6] Moses took half of the blood and put it in large bowls; the other half he splashed on the altar. [7] Taking the book of the covenant, he read it aloud to the people, who answered, "All that the LORD has said, we will heed and do." [8] Then he took the blood and sprinkled it on the people, saying, "This is the blood of the covenant that the LORD has made with you in accordance with all these words of his."

Responsorial Psalm: Psalms 116:12-13, 15-16, 17-18

*R. [13] I will take the cup of salvation, and call on
        the name of the Lord. or: Alleluia.*

[12] How shall I make a return to the LORD
        for all the good he has done for me?
[13] The cup of salvation I will take up,
        and I will call upon the name of the LORD.

*R. I will take the cup of salvation, and call on the
        name of the Lord. or: Alleluia.*

¹⁵ Precious in the eyes of the LORD
>   is the death of his faithful ones.
¹⁶ I am your servant, the son of your
>   handmaid;
>   you have loosed my bonds.
R. I will take the cup of salvation, and call on the name of the Lord. or: Alleluia.

¹⁷ To you will I offer sacrifice of thanksgiving,
>   and I will call upon the name of the LORD.
¹⁸ My vows to the LORD I will pay
>   in the presence of all his people.
R. I will take the cup of salvation, and call on the name of the Lord. or: Alleluia.

Second Reading: Hebrews 9:11-15

¹¹ Brothers and sisters: When Christ came as high priest of the good things that have come to be, passing through the greater and more perfect tabernacle not made by hands, that is, not belonging to this creation, ¹² he entered once for all into the sanctuary, not with the blood of goats and calves but with his own blood, thus obtaining eternal redemption. ¹³ For if the blood of goats and bulls and the sprinkling of a heifer's ashes can sanctify those who are defiled so that their flesh is cleansed, ¹⁴ how much more will the blood of Christ, who through the eternal Spirit offered himself unblemished to God, cleanse our consciences from dead works to worship the living God.

¹⁵ For this reason he is mediator of a new covenant: since a death has taken place for deliverance from transgressions under the first covenant, those who are called may receive the promised eternal inheritance.

Sequence - *Lauda Sion*

Laud, O Zion, your salvation,
Laud with hymns of exultation,
Christ, your king and shepherd true:

Bring him all the praise you know,
He is more than you bestow.
Never can you reach his due.

Special theme for glad thanksgiving
Is the quick'ning and the living
Bread today before you set:

From his hands of old partaken,
As we know, by faith unshaken,
Where the Twelve at supper met.

Full and clear ring out your chanting,
Joy nor sweetest grace be wanting,
From your heart let praises burst:

For today the feast is holden,
When the institution olden
Of that supper was rehearsed.

Here the new law's new oblation,
By the new king's revelation,
Ends the form of ancient rite:

Now the new the old effaces,
Truth away the shadow chases,
Light dispels the gloom of night.

What he did at supper seated,
Christ ordained to be repeated,
His memorial ne'er to cease:

And his rule for guidance taking,
Bread and wine we hallow, making
Thus our sacrifice of peace.

This the truth each Christian learns,
Bread into his flesh he turns,
To his precious blood the wine:

Sight has fail'd, nor thought conceives,
But a dauntless faith believes,
Resting on a pow'r divine.

Here beneath these signs are hidden
Priceless things to sense forbidden;
Signs, not things are all we see:

Blood is poured and flesh is broken,
Yet in either wondrous token
Christ entire we know to be.

Whoso of this food partakes,
Does not rend the Lord nor breaks;
Christ is whole to all that taste:

Thousands are, as one, receivers,
One, as thousands of believers,
Eats of him who cannot waste.

Bad and good the feast are sharing,
Of what divers dooms preparing,
Endless death, or endless life.

Life to these, to those damnation,
See how like participation
Is with unlike issues rife.

When the sacrament is broken,
Doubt not, but believe 'tis spoken,
That each sever'd outward token
doth the very whole contain.

Nought the precious gift divides,
Breaking but the sign betides
Jesus still the same abides,
still unbroken does remain.

The shorter form of the sequence begins here.

Lo! the angel's food is given
To the pilgrim who has striven;

See the children's bread from heaven,
which on dogs may not be spent.

Truth the ancient types fulfilling,
Isaac bound, a victim willing,
Paschal lamb, its lifeblood spilling,
manna to the fathers sent.

Very bread, good shepherd, tend us,
Jesu, of your love befriend us,
You refresh us, you defend us,
Your eternal goodness send us
In the land of life to see.

You who all things can and know,
Who on earth such food bestow,
Grant us with your saints, though lowest,
Where the heav'nly feast you show,
Fellow heirs and guests to be. Amen.
 Alleluia.

Alleluia: John 6:51
R. Alleluia, alleluia.
[51] I am the living bread that came down from
        heaven, says the Lord;
whoever eats this bread will live forever.
R. Alleluia, alleluia.

Gospel: Mark 14:12-16, 22-26
[12] On the first day of the Feast of Unleavened Bread, when they sacrificed the Passover lamb, Jesus' disciples said to him, "Where do you want us to go and prepare for you to eat the Passover?" [13] He sent two of his disciples and said to them, "Go into the city and a man will meet you, carrying a jar of water. Follow him. [14] Wherever he enters, say to the master of the house, 'The Teacher says, "Where is my guest room where I may eat the Passover with my disciples?"' [15] Then he will show you a large upper room furnished and ready. Make the preparations for us there." [16] The disciples then went off, entered the city, and found it just as he had told them; and they prepared the Passover.

²² While they were eating, he took bread, said the blessing, broke it, gave it to them, and said, "Take it; this is my body." ²³ Then he took a cup, gave thanks, and gave it to them, and they all drank from it. ²⁴ He said to them, "This is my blood of the covenant, which will be shed for many. ²⁵ Amen, I say to you, I shall not drink again the fruit of the vine until the day when I drink it new in the kingdom of God." ²⁶ Then, after singing a hymn, they went out to the Mount of Olives.

Sunday June 9, 2024
Tenth Sunday in Ordinary Time, Year B

First Reading: Genesis 3:9-15

[9] After the man, Adam, had eaten of the tree, the LORD God called to the man and asked him, "Where are you?" [10] He answered, "I heard you in the garden; but I was afraid, because I was naked, so I hid myself." [11] Then he asked, "Who told you that you were naked? You have eaten, then, from the tree of which I had forbidden you to eat!" [12] The man replied, "The woman whom you put here with me— she gave me fruit from the tree, and so I ate it." [13] The LORD God then asked the woman, "Why did you do such a thing?" The woman answered, "The serpent tricked me into it, so I ate it."

[14] Then the LORD God said to the serpent:

"Because you have done this, you shall be
    banned
    from all the animals
    and from all the wild creatures;
on your belly shall you crawl,
    and dirt shall you eat
    all the days of your life.
[15] I will put enmity between you and the
    woman,
    and between your offspring and hers;
he will strike at your head,
    while you strike at his heel."

Responsorial Psalm: Psalms 130:1-2, 3-4, 5-6, 7-8
R. ^(7bc) *With the Lord there is mercy, and fullness*
               of redemption.
[1] Out of the depths I cry to you, O LORD;

LORD, hear my voice!
² Let your ears be attentive
    to my voice in supplication.
**R. With the Lord there is mercy, and fullness of
    redemption.**

³ If you, O LORD, mark iniquities,
    LORD, who can stand?
⁴ But with you is forgiveness,
    that you may be revered.
**R. With the Lord there is mercy, and fullness of
    redemption.**

⁵ I trust in the LORD;
    my soul trusts in his word.
⁶ More than sentinels wait for the dawn,
    let Israel wait for the LORD.
**R. With the Lord there is mercy, and fullness of
    redemption.**

⁷ For with the LORD is kindness
    and with him is plenteous redemption
⁸ and he will redeem Israel
    from all their iniquities.
**R. With the Lord there is mercy, and fullness of
    redemption.**

Second Reading: 2 Corinthians 4:13-5:1

¹³ Brothers and sisters: Since we have the same spirit of faith, according to what is written, *I believed, therefore I spoke*, we too believe and therefore we speak,¹⁴ knowing that the one who raised the Lord Jesus will raise us also with Jesus and place us with you in his presence. ¹⁵ Everything indeed is for you, so that the grace bestowed in abundance on more and more people may cause the thanksgiving to overflow for the glory of God. ¹⁶ Therefore, we are not discouraged; rather, although our outer self is wasting away, our inner self is being renewed day by day. ¹⁷ For this momentary light affliction is producing for us an eternal weight of glory beyond all comparison, ¹⁸ as we look not to what is seen but to what is unseen; for what is seen is transitory, but what is unseen is eternal. ¹ For we know that if our earthly dwelling, a tent, should be

destroyed, we have a building from God, a dwelling not made with hands, eternal in heaven.

Alleluia: John 12:31B-32
R. Alleluia, alleluia.
31B Now the ruler of the world will be driven
out, says the Lord;
32 and when I am lifted up from the earth, I
will draw everyone to myself.
R. Alleluia, alleluia.

Gospel: Mark 3:20-35
20 Jesus came home with his disciples. Again the crowd gathered, making it impossible for them even to eat. 21 When his relatives heard of this they set out to seize him, for they said, "He is out of his mind." 22 The scribes who had come from Jerusalem said, "He is possessed by Beelzebul," and "By the prince of demons he drives out demons."

23 Summoning them, he began to speak to them in parables, "How can Satan drive out Satan? 24 If a kingdom is divided against itself, that kingdom cannot stand. 25 And if a house is divided against itself, that house will not be able to stand. 26 And if Satan has risen up against himself and is divided, he cannot stand; that is the end of him. 27 But no one can enter a strong man's house to plunder his property unless he first ties up the strong man. Then he can plunder the house. 28 Amen, I say to you, all sins and all blasphemies that people utter will be forgiven them. 29 But whoever blasphemes against the Holy Spirit will never have forgiveness, but is guilty of an everlasting sin." 30 For they had said, "He has an unclean spirit."

31 His mother and his brothers arrived. Standing outside they sent word to him and called him. 32 A crowd seated around him told him, "Your mother and your brothers and your sisters are outside asking for you." 33 But he said to them in reply, "Who are my mother and my brothers?" 34 And looking around at those seated in the circle he said, "Here are my mother and my brothers. 35 For whoever does the will of God is my brother and sister and mother."

Sunday June 16, 2024
Eleventh Sunday in Ordinary Time, Year B
First Reading: Ezekiel 17:22-24
22 Thus says the Lord GOD:

I, too, will take from the crest of the cedar,
from its topmost branches tear off a

tender shoot,
and plant it on a high and lofty mountain;
²³ on the mountain heights of Israel I will
plant it.
It shall put forth branches and bear fruit,
and become a majestic cedar.
Birds of every kind shall dwell beneath it,
every winged thing in the shade of its
boughs.
²⁴ And all the trees of the field shall know
that I, the LORD,
bring low the high tree,
lift high the lowly tree,
wither up the green tree,
and make the withered tree bloom.
As I, the LORD, have spoken, so will I do.

Responsorial Psalm: Psalms 92:2-3, 13-14, 15-16
R. (cf. 2a) Lord, it is good to give thanks to you.
² It is good to give thanks to the LORD,
to sing praise to your name, Most High,
³ To proclaim your kindness at dawn
and your faithfulness throughout the
night.
R. Lord, it is good to give thanks to you.

¹³ The just one shall flourish like the palm tree,
like a cedar of Lebanon shall he grow.
¹⁴ They that are planted in the house of the
LORD
shall flourish in the courts of our God.
R. Lord, it is good to give thanks to you.

¹⁵ They shall bear fruit even in old age;
vigorous and sturdy shall they be,
¹⁶ Declaring how just is the LORD,
my rock, in whom there is no wrong.
R. Lord, it is good to give thanks to you.

Second Reading: 2 Corinthians 5:6-10

[6] Brothers and sisters: We are always courageous, although we know that while we are at home in the body we are away from the Lord, [7] for we walk by faith, not by sight. [8] Yet we are courageous, and we would rather leave the body and go home to the Lord. [9] Therefore, we aspire to please him, whether we are at home or away. [10] For we must all appear before the judgment seat of Christ, so that each may receive recompense, according to what he did in the body, whether good or evil.

Alleluia

R. Alleluia, alleluia.

The seed is the word of God, Christ is the
        sower.

All who come to him will live for ever.

R. Alleluia, alleluia.

Gospel: Mark 4:26-34

[26] Jesus said to the crowds: "This is how it is with the kingdom of God; it is as if a man were to scatter seed on the land [27] and would sleep and rise night and day and through it all the seed would sprout and grow, he knows not how. [28] Of its own accord the land yields fruit, first the blade, then the ear, then the full grain in the ear. [29] And when the grain is ripe, he wields the sickle at once, for the harvest has come."

[30] He said, "To what shall we compare the kingdom of God, or what parable can we use for it? [31] It is like a mustard seed that, when it is sown in the ground, is the smallest of all the seeds on the earth. [32] But once it is sown, it springs up and becomes the largest of plants and puts forth large branches, so that the birds of the sky can dwell in its shade." [33] With many such parables he spoke the word to them as they were able to understand it. [34] Without parables he did not speak to them, but to his own disciples he explained everything in private.

Sunday June 23, 2024
Twelfth Sunday in Ordinary Time, Year B

First Reading: Job 38:1, 8-11

[1] The Lord addressed Job out of the storm and said:

[8] Who shut within doors the sea,
        when it burst forth from the womb;

⁹ when I made the clouds its garment
     and thick darkness its swaddling bands?
¹⁰ When I set limits for it
     and fastened the bar of its door,
¹¹ and said: Thus far shall you come but no
       farther,
     and here shall your proud waves be
       stilled!

Responsorial Psalm: Psalms 107:23-24, 25-26, 28-29, 30-31
R. ^{*(1b)*} ***Give thanks to the Lord, his love is***
       everlasting. *or:* ***Alleluia.***
²³ They who sailed the sea in ships,
     trading on the deep waters,
²⁴ These saw the works of the LORD
     and his wonders in the abyss.
R. *Give thanks to the Lord, his love is*
       everlasting. *or:* ***Alleluia.***

²⁵ His command raised up a storm wind
     which tossed its waves on high.
²⁶ They mounted up to heaven; they sank to the
       depths;
     their hearts melted away in their plight.
R. *Give thanks to the Lord, his love is*
       everlasting. *or:* ***Alleluia.***
²⁸ They cried to the LORD in their distress;
     from their straits he rescued them,
²⁹ He hushed the storm to a gentle breeze,
     and the billows of the sea were stilled.
R. *Give thanks to the Lord, his love is*
       everlasting. *or:* ***Alleluia.***

³⁰They rejoiced that they were calmed,
     and he brought them to their desired
       haven.
³¹Let them give thanks to the LORD for his
       kindness

and his wondrous deeds to the children
of men.
**R. Give thanks to the Lord, his love is
everlasting.** or: *Alleluia.*

Second Reading: 2 Corinthians 5:14-17

Brothers and sisters: [14] The love of Christ impels us, once we have come to the conviction that one died for all; therefore, all have died. [15] He indeed died for all, so that those who live might no longer live for themselves but for him who for their sake died and was raised.

[16] Consequently, from now on we regard no one according to the flesh; even if we once knew Christ according to the flesh, yet now we know him so no longer. [17] So whoever is in Christ is a new creation: the old things have passed away; behold, new things have come.

Alleluia: Luke 7:16
R. Alleluia, alleluia.
[16]A great prophet has risen in our midst,
God has visited his people.
R. Alleluia, alleluia.

Gospel: Mark 4:35-41

[35] On that day, as evening drew on, Jesus said to his disciples: "Let us cross to the other side." [36] Leaving the crowd, they took Jesus with them in the boat just as he was. And other boats were with him. [37] A violent squall came up and waves were breaking over the boat, so that it was already filling up. [38] Jesus was in the stern, asleep on a cushion. They woke him and said to him, "Teacher, do you not care that we are perishing?" [39] He woke up, rebuked the wind, and said to the sea, "Quiet! Be still!" The wind ceased and there was great calm. [40] Then he asked them, "Why are you terrified? Do you not yet have faith?" [41] They were filled with great awe and said to one another, "Who then is this whom even wind and sea obey?"

Sunday June 30, 2024
Thirteenth Sunday in Ordinary Time, Year B
First Reading: Wisdom 1:13-15; 2:23-24

[13] God did not make death,
nor does he rejoice in the destruction of
the living.

[14] For he fashioned all things that they might
      have being;
    and the creatures of the world are
      wholesome,
and there is not a destructive drug among
    them
    nor any domain of the netherworld on
      earth,
    [15] for justice is undying.
[23] For God formed man to be imperishable;
    the image of his own nature he made
      him.
[24] But by the envy of the devil, death entered
      the world,
    and they who belong to his company
      experience it.

Responsorial Psalm: Psalms 30:2, 4, 5-6, 11, 12, 13
**R. [2a] I will praise you, Lord, for you have
            rescued me.**
[2] I will extol you, O LORD, for you drew me
      clear
    and did not let my enemies rejoice over
      me.
[4] O LORD, you brought me up from the
      netherworld;
    you preserved me from among those
      going down into the pit.
**R. I will praise you, Lord, for you have rescued
            me.**

[5] Sing praise to the LORD, you his faithful ones,
    and give thanks to his holy name.
[6] For his anger lasts but a moment;
    a lifetime, his good will.
At nightfall, weeping enters in,
    but with the dawn, rejoicing.
**R. I will praise you, Lord, for you have rescued
            me.**

¹¹ Hear, O LORD, and have pity on me;
>   O LORD, be my helper.
¹² You changed my mourning into dancing;
>   ¹³ O LORD, my God, forever will I give you
>   thanks.

R. I will praise you, Lord, for you have rescued me.

Second Reading: 2 Corinthians 8:7, 9, 13-15

⁷ Brothers and sisters: As you excel in every respect, in faith, discourse, knowledge, all earnestness, and in the love we have for you, may you excel in this gracious act also.

⁹ For you know the gracious act of our Lord Jesus Christ, that though he was rich, for your sake he became poor, so that by his poverty you might become rich. ¹³ Not that others should have relief while you are burdened, but that as a matter of equality ¹⁴ your abundance at the present time should supply their needs, so that their abundance may also supply your needs, that there may be equality. ¹⁵ As it is written:

Whoever had much did not have more,
*   and whoever had little did not have less.*

Alleluia: cf. 2 Timothy 1:10
R. Alleluia, alleluia.
¹⁰Our Savior Jesus Christ destroyed death
and brought life to light through the Gospel.
R. Alleluia, alleluia.

Gospel: Mark 5:21-43

²¹ When Jesus had crossed again in the boat to the other side, a large crowd gathered around him, and he stayed close to the sea. ²² One of the synagogue officials, named Jairus, came forward. Seeing him he fell at his feet ²³ and pleaded earnestly with him, saying, "My daughter is at the point of death. Please, come lay your hands on her that she may get well and live." ²⁴ He went off with him, and a large crowd followed him and pressed upon him.

²⁵ There was a woman afflicted with hemorrhages for twelve years. ²⁶ She had suffered greatly at the hands of many doctors and had spent all that she had. Yet she was not helped but only grew worse. ²⁷ She had heard about Jesus and came up behind him in the crowd and touched his cloak.²⁸She said, "If I but touch his clothes, I shall be cured." ²⁹ Immediately her flow of blood dried up. She felt in her body that she was healed of her affliction. ³⁰ Jesus, aware at once that power had gone out from him, turned around in the crowd and asked, "Who has touched my clothes?" ³¹ But his disciples said to Jesus, "You see how the crowd is pressing upon you, and yet you ask, 'Who touched me?'" ³² And he looked around to see who had done it. ³³ The woman, realizing what had happened to her, approached in fear and trembling. She fell down before Jesus and told him the whole truth. ³⁴ He said to her, "Daughter, your faith has saved you. Go in peace and be cured of your affliction."

³⁵ While he was still speaking, people from the synagogue official's house arrived and said, "Your daughter has died; why trouble the teacher any longer?" ³⁶ Disregarding the message that was reported, Jesus said to the synagogue official, "Do not be afraid; just have faith." ³⁷ He did not allow anyone to accompany him inside except Peter, James, and John, the brother of James. ³⁸ When they arrived at the house of the synagogue official, he caught sight of a commotion, people weeping and wailing loudly. ³⁹ So he went in and said to them, "Why this commotion and weeping? The child is not dead but asleep." ⁴⁰ And they ridiculed him. Then he put them all out. He took along the child's father and mother and those who were with him and entered the room where the child was. ⁴¹ He took the child by the hand and said to her, "*Talitha koum*," which means, "Little girl, I say to you, arise!" ⁴² The girl, a child of twelve, arose immediately and walked around. At that they were utterly astounded. ⁴³ He gave strict orders that no one should know this and said that she should be given something to eat.

OR Mark 5:21-24, 35B-43

²¹ When Jesus had crossed again in the boat to the other side, a large crowd gathered around him, and he stayed close to the sea. ²² One of the synagogue officials, named Jairus, came forward. Seeing him he fell at his feet ²³ and pleaded earnestly with him, saying, "My daughter is at the point of death. Please, come lay your hands on her that she may get well and live." ²⁴ He went off with him, and a large crowd followed him and pressed upon him.

³⁵ᴮ While he was still speaking, people from the synagogue official's house arrived and said, "Your daughter has died; why trouble the teacher any longer?" ³⁶ Disregarding the message that was reported, Jesus said to the synagogue official, "Do not be afraid; just have faith." ³⁷ He did not allow anyone to accompany him inside except Peter, James, and John, the brother of James. ³⁸ When they arrived at the house

of the synagogue official, he caught sight of a commotion, people weeping and wailing loudly. [39] So he went in and said to them, "Why this commotion and weeping? The child is not dead but asleep." [40] And they ridiculed him. Then he put them all out. He took along the child's father and mother and those who were with him and entered the room where the child was. [41] He took the child by the hand and said to her, "*Talitha koum*," which means, "Little girl, I say to you, arise!"

[42] The girl, a child of twelve, arose immediately and walked around. At that they were utterly astounded. [43] He gave strict orders that no one should know this and said that she should be given something to eat.

Sunday July 7, 2024

Fourteenth Sunday in Ordinary Time, Year B
First Reading: Ezekiel 2:2-5

[2] As the LORD spoke to me, the spirit entered into me and set me on my feet, and I heard the one who was speaking [3] say to me: Son of man, I am sending you to the Israelites, rebels who have rebelled against me; they and their ancestors have revolted against me to this very day. [4] Hard of face and obstinate of heart are they to whom I am sending you. But you shall say to them: Thus says the Lord GOD! [5] And whether they heed or resist—for they are a rebellious house—they shall know that a prophet has been among them.

Responsorial Psalm: Psalms 123:1-2, 2, 3-4
R. *(2cd)* **Our eyes are fixed on the Lord, pleading**
    for his mercy.
[1] To you I lift up my eyes
    who are enthroned in heaven—
[2AB] As the eyes of servants
    are on the hands of their masters.
R. **Our eyes are fixed on the Lord, pleading for**
    his mercy.

[2BC] As the eyes of a maid
    are on the hands of her mistress,
So are our eyes on the LORD, our God,
    till he have pity on us.

*R. Our eyes are fixed on the Lord, pleading for
his mercy.*

[3] Have pity on us, O LORD, have pity on us,
for we are more than sated with
contempt;
[4] our souls are more than sated
with the mockery of the arrogant,
with the contempt of the proud.
*R. Our eyes are fixed on the Lord, pleading for
his mercy.*

Second Reading: 2 Corinthians 12:7-10

[7] Brothers and sisters: That I, Paul, might not become too elated, because of the abundance of the revelations, a thorn in the flesh was given to me, an angel of Satan, to beat me, to keep me from being too elated. [8] Three times I begged the Lord about this, that it might leave me, [9] but he said to me, "My grace is sufficient for you, for power is made perfect in weakness." I will rather boast most gladly of my weaknesses, in order that the power of Christ may dwell with me. [10] Therefore, I am content with weaknesses, insults, hardships, persecutions, and constraints, for the sake of Christ; for when I am weak, then I am strong.

Alleluia: cf. Luke 4:18

R. Alleluia, alleluia.
[18] The Spirit of the Lord is upon me
for he sent me to bring glad tidings to the
poor.
R. Alleluia, alleluia.

Gospel: Mark 6:1-6

[1] Jesus departed from there and came to his native place, accompanied by his disciples. [2] When the sabbath came he began to teach in the synagogue, and many who heard him were astonished. They said, "Where did this man get all this? What kind of wisdom has been given him? What mighty deeds are wrought by his hands! [3] Is he not the carpenter, the son of Mary, and the brother of James and Joses and Judas and Simon? And are not his sisters here with us?" And they took offense at him. [4] Jesus said to them, "A prophet is not without honor except in his native place and among his own kin and in his own house." [5] So he was not able to perform any mighty deed there,

apart from curing a few sick people by laying his hands on them. [6] He was amazed at their lack of faith.

Sunday July 14, 2024
Fifteenth Sunday in Ordinary Time, Year B

First Reading: Amos 7:12-15

[12] Amaziah, priest of Bethel, said to Amos, "Off with you, visionary, flee to the land of Judah! There earn your bread by prophesying, [13] but never again prophesy in Bethel; for it is the king's sanctuary and a royal temple."

[14] Amos answered Amaziah, "I was no prophet, nor have I belonged to a company of prophets; I was a shepherd and a dresser of sycamores. [15] The LORD took me from following the flock, and said to me, Go, prophesy to my people Israel."

Responsorial Psalm: Psalms 85:9-10, 11-12, 13-14

R. [8] *Lord, let us see your kindness, and grant*
           us your salvation.

[9] I will hear what God proclaims;
        the LORD—for he proclaims peace.
[10] Near indeed is his salvation to those who
            fear him,
        glory dwelling in our land.
R. *Lord, let us see your kindness, and grant us*
           your salvation.

[11] Kindness and truth shall meet;
        justice and peace shall kiss.
[12] Truth shall spring out of the earth,
        and justice shall look down from heaven.
R. *Lord, let us see your kindness, and grant us*
           your salvation.

[13] The LORD himself will give his benefits;
        our land shall yield its increase.
[14] Justice shall walk before him,
        and prepare the way of his steps.
R. *Lord, let us see your kindness, and grant us*
           your salvation.

Second Reading: Ephesians 1:3-14

[3] Blessed be the God and Father of our Lord Jesus Christ, who has blessed us in Christ with every spiritual blessing in the heavens, [4] as he chose us in him, before the foundation of the world, to be holy and without blemish before him. In love [5] he destined us for adoption to himself through Jesus Christ, in accord with the favor of his will, [6] for the praise of the glory of his grace that he granted us in the beloved. [7] In him we have redemption by his blood, the forgiveness of transgressions, in accord with the riches of his grace [8] that he lavished upon us. In all wisdom and insight, [9] he has made known to us the mystery of his will in accord with his favor that he set forth in him [10] as a plan for the fullness of times, to sum up all things in Christ, in heaven and on earth.

[11] In him we were also chosen, destined in accord with the purpose of the One who accomplishes all things according to the intention of his will, [12] so that we might exist for the praise of his glory, we who first hoped in Christ. [13] In him you also, who have heard the word of truth, the gospel of your salvation, and have believed in him, were sealed with the promised Holy Spirit, [14] which is the first installment of our inheritance toward redemption as God's possession, to the praise of his glory.

Or Ephesians 1:3-10

[3] Blessed be the God and Father of our Lord Jesus Christ, who has blessed us in Christ with every spiritual blessing in the heavens, [4] as he chose us in him, before the foundation of the world, to be holy and without blemish before him. In love [5] he destined us for adoption to himself through Jesus Christ, in accord with the favor of his will, [6] for the praise of the glory of his grace that he granted us in the beloved.

[7] In him we have redemption by his blood, the forgiveness of transgressions, in accord with the riches of his grace [8] that he lavished upon us. In all wisdom and insight, [9] he has made known to us the mystery of his will in accord with his favor that he set forth in him [10] as a plan for the fullness of times, to sum up all things in Christ, in heaven and on earth.

Alleluia: cf. Ephesians 1:17-18
R. Alleluia, alleluia.
[17] May the Father of our Lord Jesus Christ
enlighten the eyes of our hearts,
[18] that we may know what is the hope
that belongs to our call.
R. Alleluia, alleluia.

Gospel: Mark 6:7-13

[7] Jesus summoned the Twelve and began to send them out two by two and gave them authority over unclean spirits. [8] He instructed them to take nothing for the journey but a walking stick—no food, no sack, no money in their belts. [9] They were, however, to wear sandals but not a second tunic. [10] He said to them, "Wherever you enter a house, stay there until you leave. [11] Whatever place does not welcome you or listen to you, leave there and shake the dust off your feet in testimony against them." [12] So they went off and preached repentance. [13] The Twelve drove out many demons, and they anointed with oil many who were sick and cured them.

Sunday July 21, 2024

Sixteenth Sunday in Ordinary Time, Year B

First Reading: Jeremiah 23:1-6

[1] Woe to the shepherds
>   who mislead and scatter the flock of my
>   pasture,
>   says the LORD.

[2] Therefore, thus says the LORD, the God of
>   Israel,
>   against the shepherds who shepherd my
>   people:
>   You have scattered my sheep and driven
>   them away.

You have not cared for them,
>   but I will take care to punish your evil
>   deeds.

[3] I myself will gather the remnant of my flock
>   from all the lands to which I have driven
>   them
>   and bring them back to their meadow;
>   there they shall increase and multiply.

[4] I will appoint shepherds for them who will
>   shepherd them
>   so that they need no longer fear and
>   tremble;
>   and none shall be missing, says the LORD.

>   [5] Behold, the days are coming, says the
>   LORD,

when I will raise up a righteous shoot to
    David;
as king he shall reign and govern wisely,
he shall do what is just and right in the
    land.
[6] In his days Judah shall be saved,
Israel shall dwell in security.
This is the name they give him:
"The LORD our justice."

Responsorial Psalm: Psalms 23:1-3, 3-4, 5, 6
R. [(1)] *The Lord is my shepherd; there is nothing I*
    shall want.
[1] The LORD is my shepherd; I shall not want.
    [2] In verdant pastures he gives me repose;
beside restful waters he leads me;
    [3A] he refreshes my soul.
R. *The Lord is my shepherd; there is nothing I*
    shall want.

[3B] He guides me in right paths
    for his name's sake.
[4] Even though I walk in the dark valley
    I fear no evil; for you are at my side
with your rod and your staff
    that give me courage.
R. *The Lord is my shepherd; there is nothing I*
    shall want.

[5] You spread the table before me
    in the sight of my foes;
you anoint my head with oil;
    my cup overflows.
R. *The Lord is my shepherd; there is nothing I*
    shall want.

[6] Only goodness and kindness follow me
    all the days of my life;
and I shall dwell in the house of the LORD

for years to come.

R. The Lord is my shepherd; there is nothing I
shall want.

Second Reading: Ephesians 2:13-18
[13] Brothers and sisters: In Christ Jesus you who once were far off have become near by the blood of Christ.

[14] For he is our peace, he who made both one and broke down the dividing wall of enmity, through his flesh, [15] abolishing the law with its commandments and legal claims, that he might create in himself one new person in place of the two, thus establishing peace, [16] and might reconcile both with God, in one body, through the cross, putting that enmity to death by it. [17] He came and preached peace to you who were far off and peace to those who were near, [18] for through him we both have access in one Spirit to the Father.

Alleluia: John 10:27
R. Alleluia, alleluia.
[27] My sheep hear my voice, says the Lord;
I know them, and they follow me.
R. Alleluia, alleluia.

Gospel: Mark 6:30-34
[30] The apostles gathered together with Jesus and reported all they had done and taught. [31] He said to them, "Come away by yourselves to a deserted place and rest a while." People were coming and going in great numbers, and they had no opportunity even to eat. [32] So they went off in the boat by themselves to a deserted place. [33] People saw them leaving and many came to know about it. They hastened there on foot from all the towns and arrived at the place before them.

[34] When he disembarked and saw the vast crowd, his heart was moved with pity for them, for they were like sheep without a shepherd; and he began to teach them many things.

Sunday July 28, 2024
Seventeenth Sunday in Ordinary Time Year B
First Reading: 2 Kings 4:42-44
[42] A man came from Baal-shalishah bringing to Elisha, the man of God, twenty barley loaves made from the firstfruits, and fresh grain in the ear. Elisha said, "Give it to the people to eat." [43] But his servant objected, "How can I set this before a hundred people?" Elisha insisted, "Give it to the people to eat." "For thus says the

LORD, 'They shall eat and there shall be some left over.'" [44] And when they had eaten, there was some left over, as the LORD had said.

Responsorial Psalm: Psalms 145:10-11, 15-16, 17-18

R. *(cf. 16)* **The hand of the Lord feeds us; he**
                    answers all our needs.

[10] Let all your works give you thanks, O LORD,
        and let your faithful ones bless you.
[11] Let them discourse of the glory of your
            kingdom
        and speak of your might.

R. **The hand of the Lord feeds us; he answers all**
            our needs.

[15] The eyes of all look hopefully to you,
        and you give them their food in due
            season;
[16] you open your hand
        and satisfy the desire of every living
            thing.

R. **The hand of the Lord feeds us; he answers all**
            our needs.

[17] The LORD is just in all his ways
        and holy in all his works.
[16] The LORD is near to all who call upon him,
        to all who call upon him in truth.

R. **The hand of the Lord feeds us; he answers all**
            our needs.

Second Reading: Ephesians 4:1-6

Brothers and sisters: [1] I, a prisoner for the Lord, urge you to live in a manner worthy of the call you have received, [2] with all humility and gentleness, with patience, bearing with one another through love, [3] striving to preserve the unity of the spirit through the bond of peace: [4] one body and one Spirit, as you were also called to the one hope of your call; [5] one Lord, one faith, one baptism; [6] one God and Father of all, who is over all and through all and in all.

Alleluia: Luke 7:16

R. Alleluia, alleluia.
[16] A great prophet has risen in our midst.
God has visited his people.
R. Alleluia, alleluia.

Gospel: John 6:1-15

[1] Jesus went across the Sea of Galilee. [2] A large crowd followed him, because they saw the signs he was performing on the sick. [3] Jesus went up on the mountain, and there he sat down with his disciples. [4] The Jewish feast of Passover was near. [5] When Jesus raised his eyes and saw that a large crowd was coming to him, he said to Philip, "Where can we buy enough food for them to eat?" [6] He said this to test him, because he himself knew what he was going to do. [7] Philip answered him, "Two hundred days' wages worth of food would not be enough for each of them to have a little." [8] One of his disciples, Andrew, the brother of Simon Peter, said to him, [9] "There is a boy here who has five barley loaves and two fish; but what good are these for so many?" [10] Jesus said, "Have the people recline." Now there was a great deal of grass in that place. So the men reclined, about five thousand in number. [11] Then Jesus took the loaves, gave thanks, and distributed them to those who were reclining, and also as much of the fish as they wanted. [12] When they had had their fill, he said to his disciples, "Gather the fragments left over, so that nothing will be wasted." [13] So they collected them, and filled twelve wicker baskets with fragments from the five barley loaves that had been more than they could eat. [14] When the people saw the sign he had done, they said, "This is truly the Prophet, the one who is to come into the world." [15] Since Jesus knew that they were going to come and carry him off to make him king, he withdrew again to the mountain alone.

Sunday August 4, 2024
Eighteenth Sunday in Ordinary Time, Year B
First Reading: Exodus 16:2-4, 12-15

[2] The whole Israelite community grumbled against Moses and Aaron. [3] The Israelites said to them, "Would that we had died at the LORD's hand in the land of Egypt, as we sat by our fleshpots and ate our fill of bread! But you had to lead us into this desert to make the whole community die of famine!"

[4] Then the LORD said to Moses, "I will now rain down bread from heaven for you. Each day the people are to go out and gather their daily portion; thus will I test them, to see whether they follow my instructions or not.

[12] "I have heard the grumbling of the Israelites. Tell them: In the evening twilight you shall eat flesh, and in the morning you shall have your fill of bread, so that you may know that I, the LORD, am your God."

[13] In the evening quail came up and covered the camp. In the morning a dew lay all about the camp, [14] and when the dew evaporated, there on the surface of the desert were fine flakes like hoarfrost on the ground. [15] On seeing it, the Israelites asked one another, "What is this?" for they did not know what it was. But Moses told them, "This is the bread that the LORD has given you to eat."

Responsorial Psalm: Psalms 78:3-4, 23-24, 25, 54

R. [24b] *The Lord gave them bread from heaven.*

[3] What we have heard and know,
    and what our fathers have declared to us,
[4] We will declare to the generation to come
    the glorious deeds of the LORD and his
      strength
    and the wonders that he wrought.

R. *The Lord gave them bread from heaven.*

[23] He commanded the skies above
    and opened the doors of heaven;
[24] he rained manna upon them for food
    and gave them heavenly bread.

R. *The Lord gave them bread from heaven.*

[25] Man ate the bread of angels,
    food he sent them in abundance.
[54] And he brought them to his holy land,
    to the mountains his right hand had won.

R. *The Lord gave them bread from heaven.*

Second Reading: Ephesians 4:17, 20-24

Brothers and sisters: [17] I declare and testify in the Lord that you must no longer live as the Gentiles do, in the futility of their minds; [20] that is not how you learned Christ, [21] assuming that you have heard of him and were taught in him, as truth is in Jesus, [22] that you should put away the old self of your former way of life, corrupted through deceitful desires, [23] and be renewed in the spirit of your minds, [24] and put on the new self, created in God's way in righteousness and holiness of truth.

Alleluia: Matthew 4:4B

R. Alleluia, alleluia.

⁴ᴮ One does not live on bread alone, but on

every

word that comes forth from the mouth of

God.

R. Alleluia, alleluia.

Gospel: John 6:24-35

²⁴ When the crowd saw that neither Jesus nor his disciples were there, they themselves got into boats and came to Capernaum looking for Jesus. ²⁵ And when they found him across the sea they said to him, "Rabbi, when did you get here?" ²⁶ Jesus answered them and said, "Amen, amen, I say to you, you are looking for me not because you saw signs but because you ate the loaves and were filled. ²⁷ Do not work for food that perishes but for the food that endures for eternal life, which the Son of Man will give you. For on him the Father, God, has set his seal." ²⁸ So they said to him, "What can we do to accomplish the works of God?" ²⁹ Jesus answered and said to them, "This is the work of God, that you believe in the one he sent." ³⁰ So they said to him, "What sign can you do, that we may see and believe in you? What can you do? ³¹ Our ancestors ate manna in the desert, as it is written: *He gave them bread from heaven to eat*." ³² So Jesus said to them, "Amen, amen, I say to you, it was not Moses who gave the bread from heaven; my Father gives you the true bread from heaven. ³³ For the bread of God is that which comes down from heaven and gives life to the world."

³⁴ So they said to him, "Sir, give us this bread always." ³⁵ Jesus said to them, "I am the bread of life; whoever comes to me will never hunger, and whoever believes in me will never thirst."

Sunday August 11, 2024
Nineteenth Sunday in Ordinary Time, Year B
First Reading: 1 Kings 19:4-8

⁴ Elijah went a day's journey into the desert, until he came to a broom tree and sat beneath it. He prayed for death saying: "This is enough, O LORD! Take my life, for I am no better than my fathers." ⁵ He lay down and fell asleep under the broom tree, but then an angel touched him and ordered him to get up and eat. ⁶ Elijah looked and there at his head was a hearth cake and a jug of water. After he ate and drank, he lay down again, ⁷ but the angel of the LORD came back a second time, touched him, and ordered, "Get up and eat, else the journey will be too long for you!" ⁸ He got up, ate, and drank; then strengthened by that food, he walked forty days and forty nights to the mountain of God, Horeb.

Responsorial Psalm: Psalms 34:2-3, 4-5, 6-7, 8-9

R. *(9a) Taste and see the goodness of the Lord.*

2 I will bless the LORD at all times;
  his praise shall be ever in my mouth.
3 Let my soul glory in the LORD;
  the lowly will hear me and be glad.

R. Taste and see the goodness of the Lord.

4 Glorify the LORD with me,
  let us together extol his name.
5 I sought the LORD, and he answered me
  and delivered me from all my fears.

R. Taste and see the goodness of the Lord.

6 Look to him that you may be radiant with
    joy,
  and your faces may not blush with
    shame.
7 When the afflicted man called out, the LORD
    heard,
  and from all his distress he saved him.

R. Taste and see the goodness of the Lord.

8 The angel of the LORD encamps
  around those who fear him and delivers
    them.
9 Taste and see how good the LORD is;
  blessed the man who takes refuge in him.

R. Taste and see the goodness of the Lord.

Second Reading: Ephesians 4:30-5:2

Brothers and sisters: 30 Do not grieve the Holy Spirit of God, with which you were sealed for the day of redemption. 31 All bitterness, fury, anger, shouting, and reviling must be removed from you, along with all malice. 32 And be kind to one another, compassionate, forgiving one another as God has forgiven you in Christ.

1 So be imitators of God, as beloved children, 2 and live in love, as Christ loved us and handed himself over for us as a sacrificial offering to God for a fragrant aroma.

Alleluia: John 6:51
R. Alleluia, alleluia.
[51] I am the living bread that came down from
heaven, says the Lord;
whoever eats this bread will live forever.
R. Alleluia, alleluia.

Gospel: John 6:41-51
[41] The Jews murmured about Jesus because he said, "I am the bread that came down from heaven," [42] and they said, "Is this not Jesus, the son of Joseph? Do we not know his father and mother? Then how can he say, 'I have come down from heaven'?" [43] Jesus answered and said to them, "Stop murmuring among yourselves. [44] No one can come to me unless the Father who sent me draw him, and I will raise him on the last day. [45] It is written in the prophets:

They shall all be taught by God.

Everyone who listens to my Father and learns from him comes to me. [46] Not that anyone has seen the Father except the one who is from God; he has seen the Father. [47] Amen, amen, I say to you, whoever believes has eternal life. [48] I am the bread of life. [49] Your ancestors ate the manna in the desert, but they died; [50] this is the bread that comes down from heaven so that one may eat it and not die. [51] I am the living bread that came down from heaven; whoever eats this bread will live forever; and the bread that I will give is my flesh for the life of the world."

Sunday August 18, 2024
Twentieth Saturday in Ordinary Time, Year B
First Reading: Proverbs 9:1-6
[1] Wisdom has built her house,
she has set up her seven columns;
[2] she has dressed her meat, mixed her wine,
yes, she has spread her table.
[3] She has sent out her maidens; she calls
from the heights out over the city:
[4] "Let whoever is simple turn in here";
to the one who lacks understanding, she
says,
[5] "Come, eat of my food,
and drink of the wine I have mixed!

[6] Forsake foolishness that you may live;
>   advance in the way of understanding."

Responsorial Psalm: Psalms 34:2-3, 4-5, 6-7

R. *(9a)* *Taste and see the goodness of the Lord.*

[2] I will bless the LORD at all times;
>   his praise shall be ever in my mouth.

[3] Let my soul glory in the LORD;
>   the lowly will hear me and be glad.

R. *Taste and see the goodness of the Lord.*

[4] Glorify the LORD with me,
>   let us together extol his name.

[5] I sought the LORD, and he answered me
>   and delivered me from all my fears.

R. *Taste and see the goodness of the Lord.*

[6] Look to him that you may be radiant with
>   joy,
>   and your faces may not blush with
>   shame.

[7] When the poor one called out, the LORD
>   heard,
>   and from all his distress he saved him.

R. *Taste and see the goodness of the Lord.*

Second Reading: Ephesians 5:15-20

Brothers and sisters: [15] Watch carefully how you live, not as foolish persons but as wise, [16] making the most of the opportunity, because the days are evil. [17] Therefore, do not continue in ignorance, but try to understand what is the will of the Lord. [18] And do not get drunk on wine, in which lies debauchery, but be filled with the Spirit, [19] addressing one another in psalms and hymns and spiritual songs, singing and playing to the Lord in your hearts, [20] giving thanks always and for everything in the name of our Lord Jesus Christ to God the Father.

Alleluia: John 6:56

R. Alleluia, alleluia.

[56] Whoever eats my flesh and drinks my blood remains in me and I in him, says the Lord.

R. Alleluia, alleluia.

Gospel: John 6:51-58

Jesus said to the crowds: ⁵¹ "I am the living bread that came down from heaven; whoever eats this bread will live forever; and the bread that I will give is my flesh for the life of the world."

⁵² The Jews quarreled among themselves, saying, "How can this man give us his flesh to eat?" ⁵³ Jesus said to them, "Amen, amen, I say to you, unless you eat the flesh of the Son of Man and drink his blood, you do not have life within you. ⁵⁴ Whoever eats my flesh and drinks my blood has eternal life, and I will raise him on the last day. ⁵⁵ For my flesh is true food, and my blood is true drink. ⁵⁶ Whoever eats my flesh and drinks my blood remains in me and I in him. ⁵⁷ Just as the living Father sent me and I have life because of the Father, so also the one who feeds on me will have life because of me. ⁵⁸ This is the bread that came down from heaven. Unlike your ancestors who ate and still died, whoever eats this bread will live forever."

Sunday August 25, 2024
Twenty-first Sunday in Ordinary Time Year B
First Reading: Joshua 24:1-2A, 15-17, 18B

¹ Joshua gathered together all the tribes of Israel at Shechem, summoning their elders, their leaders, their judges, and their officers. When they stood in ranks before God, ²ᴬ Joshua addressed all the people: ¹⁵ "If it does not please you to serve the LORD, decide today whom you will serve, the gods your fathers served beyond the River or the gods of the Amorites in whose country you are now dwelling. As for me and my household, we will serve the LORD."

¹⁶ But the people answered, "Far be it from us to forsake the LORD for the service of other gods. ¹⁷ For it was the LORD, our God, who brought us and our fathers up out of the land of Egypt, out of a state of slavery. He performed those great miracles before our very eyes and protected us along our entire journey and among the peoples through whom we passed. ¹⁸ᴮ Therefore we also will serve the LORD, for he is our God."

Responsorial Psalm: Psalms 34:2-3, 16-17, 18-19, 20-21
R. *⁽⁹ᵃ⁾* **Taste and see the goodness of the Lord.**

² I will bless the LORD at all times;
    his praise shall be ever in my mouth.
³ Let my soul glory in the LORD;
    the lowly will hear me and be glad.

R. Taste and see the goodness of the Lord.

[16] The LORD has eyes for the just,
    and ears for their cry.
[17] The LORD confronts the evildoers,
    to destroy remembrance of them from
        the earth.
R. Taste and see the goodness of the Lord.

[18] When the just cry out, the LORD hears them,
    and from all their distress he rescues
        them.
[19] The LORD is close to the brokenhearted;
    and those who are crushed in spirit he
        saves.
R. Taste and see the goodness of the Lord.

[20] Many are the troubles of the just one,
    but out of them all the LORD delivers him;
[21] he watches over all his bones;
    not one of them shall be broken.
R. Taste and see the goodness of the Lord.

Second Reading: Ephesians 5:21-32

Brothers and sisters: [21] Be subordinate to one another out of reverence for Christ. [22] Wives should be subordinate to their husbands as to the Lord. [23] For the husband is head of his wife just as Christ is head of the church, he himself the savior of the body. [24] As the church is subordinate to Christ, so wives should be subordinate to their husbands in everything. [25] Husbands, love your wives, even as Christ loved the church and handed himself over for her [26] to sanctify her, cleansing her by the bath of water with the word, [27] that he might present to himself the church in splendor, without spot or wrinkle or any such thing, that she might be holy and without blemish. [28] So also husbands should love their wives as their own bodies. He who loves his wife loves himself. [29] For no one hates his own flesh but rather nourishes and cherishes it, even as Christ does the church, [30] because we are members of his body. [31] *For this reason a man shall leave his father and his mother and be joined to his wife, and the two shall become one flesh*. [32] This is a great mystery, but I speak in reference to Christ and the church.

OR Ephesians 5:2A, 25-32

Brothers and sisters: [2A] Live in love, as Christ loved us. [25] Husbands, love your wives, even as Christ loved the church and handed himself over for her [26] to sanctify her, cleansing her by the bath of water with the word, [27] that he might present to himself the church in splendor, without spot or wrinkle or any such thing, that she might be holy and without blemish. [28] So also husbands should love their wives as their own bodies. He who loves his wife loves himself. [29] For no one hates his own flesh but rather nourishes and cherishes it, even as Christ does the church, [30] because we are members of his body. [31] *For this reason a man shall leave his father and his mother and be joined to his wife, and the two shall become one flesh*. [32] This is a great mystery, but I speak in reference to Christ and the church.

Alleluia: John 6:63C, 68C
R. Alleluia, alleluia.
[63C] Your words, Lord, are Spirit and life;
[68C] you have the words of everlasting life.
R. Alleluia, alleluia.

Gospel: John 6:60-69
[60] Many of Jesus' disciples who were listening said, "This saying is hard; who can accept it?" [61] Since Jesus knew that his disciples were murmuring about this, he said to them, "Does this shock you? [62] What if you were to see the Son of Man ascending to where he was before? [63] It is the spirit that gives life, while the flesh is of no avail. The words I have spoken to you are Spirit and life. [64] But there are some of you who do not believe." Jesus knew from the beginning the ones who would not believe and the one who would betray him. [65] And he said, "For this reason I have told you that no one can come to me unless it is granted him by my Father."

[66] As a result of this, many of his disciples returned to their former way of life and no longer accompanied him. [67] Jesus then said to the Twelve, "Do you also want to leave?" [68] Simon Peter answered him, "Master, to whom shall we go? You have the words of eternal life. [69] We have come to believe and are convinced that you are the Holy One of God."

Sunday September 1, 2024
Twenty-second Sunday in ordinary Time, Year B
First Reading: Deuteronomy 4:1-2, 6-8
Moses said to the people: [1] "Now, Israel, hear the statutes and decrees which I am teaching you to observe, that you may live, and may enter in and take possession of the land which the LORD, the God of your fathers, is giving you. [2] In your observance of the commandments of the LORD, your God, which I enjoin upon

you, you shall not add to what I command you nor subtract from it. [6] Observe them carefully, for thus will you give evidence of your wisdom and intelligence to the nations, who will hear of all these statutes and say, 'This great nation is truly a wise and intelligent people.' [7] For what great nation is there that has gods so close to it as the LORD, our God, is to us whenever we call upon him? [8] Or what great nation has statutes and decrees that are as just as this whole law which I am setting before you today?"

Responsorial Psalm: Psalms 15:2-3, 3-4, 4-5
R. [1a] *The one who does justice will live in the presence of the Lord.*

[2] Whoever walks blamelessly and does justice;
who thinks the truth in his heart
[3A] and slanders not with his tongue.
R. *The one who does justice will live in the presence of the Lord.*

[3B] Who harms not his fellow man,
nor takes up a reproach against his neighbor;
[4A] by whom the reprobate is despised,
while he honors those who fear the LORD.
R. *The one who does justice will live in the presence of the Lord.*

[5] Who lends not his money at usury
and accepts no bribe against the innocent.
Whoever does these things
shall never be disturbed.
R. *The one who does justice will live in the presence of the Lord.*

Second Reading: James 1:17-18, 21B-22, 27
Dearest brothers and sisters: [17] All good giving and every perfect gift is from above, coming down from the Father of lights, with whom there is no alteration or shadow caused by change. [18] He willed to give us birth by the word of truth that we may be a kind of firstfruits of his creatures.

^{21B} Humbly welcome the word that has been planted in you and is able to save your souls.

^{22} Be doers of the word and not hearers only, deluding yourselves.

^{27} Religion that is pure and undefiled before God and the Father is this: to care for orphans and widows in their affliction and to keep oneself unstained by the world.

Alleluia: James 1:18
R. Alleluia, alleluia.
^{18} The Father willed to give us birth by the
         word of truth
that we may be a kind of firstfruits of his
         creatures.
R. Alleluia, alleluia.

Gospel: Mark 7:1-8, 14-15, 21-23
^{1} When the Pharisees with some scribes who had come from Jerusalem gathered around Jesus, ^{2} they observed that some of his disciples ate their meals with unclean, that is, unwashed, hands. ^{3}—For the Pharisees and, in fact, all Jews, do not eat without carefully washing their hands, keeping the tradition of the elders. ^{4} And on coming from the marketplace they do not eat without purifying themselves. And there are many other things that they have traditionally observed, the purification of cups and jugs and kettles and beds.— ^{5} So the Pharisees and scribes questioned him, "Why do your disciples not follow the tradition of the elders but instead eat a meal with unclean hands?" ^{6} He responded, "Well did Isaiah prophesy about you hypocrites, as it is written:
This people honors me with their lips,
    but their hearts are far from me;
^{7} *in vain do they worship me,*
    teaching as doctrines human precepts.

^{8} You disregard God's commandment but cling to human tradition." ^{14} He summoned the crowd again and said to them, "Hear me, all of you, and understand. ^{15} Nothing that enters one from outside can defile that person; but the things that come out from within are what defile.

^{21} "From within people, from their hearts, come evil thoughts, unchastity, theft, murder, ^{22} adultery, greed, malice, deceit, licentiousness, envy, blasphemy, arrogance, folly. ^{23} All these evils come from within and they defile."

Sunday September 8, 2024

Twenty-third Sunday in Ordinary Time, Year B

First Reading: Isaiah 35:4-7A

Thus says the LORD:

[4] Say to those whose hearts are frightened:
>   Be strong, fear not!
Here is your God,
>   he comes with vindication;
with divine recompense
>   he comes to save you.
[5] Then will the eyes of the blind be opened,
>   the ears of the deaf be cleared;
[6] then will the lame leap like a stag,
>   then the tongue of the mute will sing.
Streams will burst forth in the desert,
>   and rivers in the steppe.
[7] The burning sands will become pools,
>   and the thirsty ground, springs of water.

Responsorial Psalm: Psalms 146:6-7, 8-9, 9-10

R. (1b) *Praise the Lord, my soul!* or: *Alleluia.*

[6] The God of Jacob keeps faith forever,
>   [7] secures justice for the oppressed,
>   gives food to the hungry.
The LORD sets captives free.
R. *Praise the Lord, my soul!* or: *Alleluia.*

[8] The LORD gives sight to the blind;
>   the LORD raises up those who were bowed
>   down.
The LORD loves the just;
>   [9A] the LORD protects strangers.
R. *Praise the Lord, my soul!* or: *Alleluia.*

[9B] The fatherless and the widow the LORD
>   sustains,
>   but the way of the wicked he thwarts.
[10] The LORD shall reign forever;
>   your God, O Zion, through all generations.
Alleluia.

R. Praise the Lord, my soul! or: **Alleluia.**

Second Reading: James 2:1-5

[1] My brothers and sisters, show no partiality as you adhere to the faith in our glorious Lord Jesus Christ. [2] For if a man with gold rings and fine clothes comes into your assembly, and a poor person in shabby clothes also comes in, [3] and you pay attention to the one wearing the fine clothes and say, "Sit here, please, " while you say to the poor one, "Stand there, " or "Sit at my feet, " [4] have you not made distinctions among yourselves and become judges with evil designs?

[5] Listen, my beloved brothers and sisters. Did not God choose those who are poor in the world to be rich in faith and heirs of the kingdom that he promised to those who love him?

Alleluia: cf. Matthew 4:23

R. Alleluia, alleluia.

[23] Jesus proclaimed the Gospel of the kingdom
and cured every disease among the people.

R. Alleluia, alleluia.

Gospel: Mark 7:31-37

[31] Again Jesus left the district of Tyre and went by way of Sidon to the Sea of Galilee, into the district of the Decapolis. [32] And people brought to him a deaf man who had a speech impediment and begged him to lay his hand on him. [33] He took him off by himself away from the crowd. He put his finger into the man's ears and, spitting, touched his tongue; [34] then he looked up to heaven and groaned, and said to him, "*Ephphatha*!" —that is, "Be opened!"— [35] And immediately the man's ears were opened, his speech impediment was removed, and he spoke plainly. [36] He ordered them not to tell anyone. But the more he ordered them not to, the more they proclaimed it. [37] They were exceedingly astonished and they said, "He has done all things well. He makes the deaf hear and the mute speak."

Sunday September 15, 2024

Twenty-fourth Sunday in Ordinary Time, Year B

First Reading: Isaiah 50:5-9A

[5] The Lord GOD opens my ear that I may hear;
and I have not rebelled,
    have not turned back.
[6] I gave my back to those who beat me,
    my cheeks to those who plucked my

beard;
my face I did not shield
    from buffets and spitting.

[7] The Lord GOD is my help,
    therefore I am not disgraced;
I have set my face like flint,
    knowing that I shall not be put to shame.
[8] He is near who upholds my right;
    if anyone wishes to oppose me,
    let us appear together.
Who disputes my right?
    Let that man confront me.
[9A] See, the Lord GOD is my help;
    who will prove me wrong?

Responsorial Psalm: Psalms 116:1-2, 3-4, 5-6, 8-9
R. [(9)] *I will walk before the Lord, in the land of the*
                living. or: *Alleluia.*
[1] I love the LORD because he has heard
    my voice in supplication,
[2] because he has inclined his ear to me
    the day I called.
R. *I will walk before the Lord, in the land of the*
        living. or: *Alleluia.*

[3] The cords of death encompassed me;
    the snares of the netherworld seized
        upon me;
    [4] I fell into distress and sorrow,
and I called upon the name of the LORD,
    "O LORD, save my life!"
R. *I will walk before the Lord, in the land of the*
        living. or: *Alleluia.*

[5] Gracious is the LORD and just;
    yes, our God is merciful.
[6] The LORD keeps the little ones;
    I was brought low, and he saved me.

**R. I will walk before the Lord, in the land of the
living.** or: *Alleluia.*

⁸ For he has freed my soul from death,
　　my eyes from tears, my feet from
　　　stumbling.
⁹ I shall walk before the LORD
　　in the land of the living.
**R. I will walk before the Lord, in the land of the
living.** or: *Alleluia.*

Second Reading: James 2:14-18

¹⁴ What good is it, my brothers and sisters, if someone says he has faith but does not have works? Can that faith save him? ¹⁵ If a brother or sister has nothing to wear and has no food for the day, ¹⁷ and one of you says to them, "Go in peace, keep warm, and eat well, " but you do not give them the necessities of the body, what good is it? So also faith of itself, if it does not have works, is dead.

¹⁸ Indeed someone might say, "You have faith and I have works." Demonstrate your faith to me without works, and I will demonstrate my faith to you from my works.

Alleluia: Galatians 6:14

R. Alleluia, alleluia.

¹⁴ May I never boast except in the cross of our
　　　Lord
through which the world has been crucified
　　　to me and I to the world.

R. Alleluia, alleluia.

Gospel: Mark 8:27-35

²⁷ Jesus and his disciples set out for the villages of Caesarea Philippi. Along the way he asked his disciples, "Who do people say that I am?" ²⁸ They said in reply, "John the Baptist, others Elijah, still others one of the prophets." ²⁹ And he asked them, "But who do you say that I am?" Peter said to him in reply, "You are the Christ." ³⁰ Then he warned them not to tell anyone about him.

³¹ He began to teach them that the Son of Man must suffer greatly and be rejected by the elders, the chief priests, and the scribes, and be killed, and rise after three days. ³² He spoke this openly. Then Peter took him aside and began to rebuke him. ³³ At this he turned around and, looking at his disciples, rebuked Peter and said, "Get behind me, Satan. You are thinking not as God does, but as human beings do."

[34] He summoned the crowd with his disciples and said to them, "Whoever wishes to come after me must deny himself, take up his cross, and follow me. [35] For whoever wishes to save his life will lose it, but whoever loses his life for my sake and that of the gospel will save it."

Sunday September 22, 2024
Twenty-fifth Sunday in Ordinary Time, Year B

First Reading: Wisdom 2:12, 17-20

The wicked say:

[12] Let us beset the just one, because he is
    obnoxious to us;
  he sets himself against our doings,
reproaches us for transgressions of the law
    and charges us with violations of our
      training.
[17] Let us see whether his words be true;
  let us find out what will happen to him.
[18] For if the just one be the son of God, God will
      defend him
  and deliver him from the hand of his
      foes.
[19] With revilement and torture let us put the
      just one to the test
  that we may have proof of his gentleness
  and try his patience.
[20] Let us condemn him to a shameful death;
  for according to his own words, God will
      take care of him.

Responsial Psalm: Psalms 54:3-4, 5, 6 AND 8

R. *(6b)* *The Lord upholds my life.*

[3] O God, by your name save me,
  and by your might defend my cause.
[4] O God, hear my prayer;
  hearken to the words of my mouth.

R. *The Lord upholds my life.*

[5] For the haughty men have risen up against me,
  the ruthless seek my life;

they set not God before their eyes.
R. The Lord upholds my life.

⁶ Behold, God is my helper;
　　the Lord sustains my life.
⁸ Freely will I offer you sacrifice;
　　I will praise your name, O LORD, for its
　　　　goodness.
R. The Lord upholds my life.

Second Reading: James 3:16-4:3

Beloved: ¹⁶ Where jealousy and selfish ambition exist, there is disorder and every foul practice. ¹⁷ But the wisdom from above is first of all pure, then peaceable, gentle, compliant, full of mercy and good fruits, without inconstancy or insincerity. ¹⁸ And the fruit of righteousness is sown in peace for those who cultivate peace.

¹ Where do the wars and where do the conflicts among you come from? Is it not from your passions that make war within your members? ² You covet but do not possess. You kill and envy but you cannot obtain; you fight and wage war. You do not possess because you do not ask. ³ You ask but do not receive, because you ask wrongly, to spend it on your passions.

Alleluia: cf. 2 Thessalonians 2:14

R. Alleluia, alleluia.
¹⁴ God has called us through the Gospel
to possess the glory of our Lord Jesus Christ.
R. Alleluia, alleluia.

Gospel: Mark 9:30-37

³⁰ Jesus and his disciples left from there and began a journey through Galilee, but he did not wish anyone to know about it. ³¹ He was teaching his disciples and telling them, "The Son of Man is to be handed over to men and they will kill him, and three days after his death the Son of Man will rise." ³² But they did not understand the saying, and they were afraid to question him.

³³ They came to Capernaum and, once inside the house, he began to ask them, "What were you arguing about on the way?" ³⁴ But they remained silent. They had been discussing among themselves on the way who was the greatest. ³⁵ Then he sat down, called the Twelve, and said to them, "If anyone wishes to be first, he shall be the last of all and the servant of all." ³⁶ Taking a child, he placed it in their midst, and putting his arms around it, he said to them, ³⁷ "Whoever

receives one child such as this in my name, receives me; and whoever receives me, receives not me but the One who sent me."

Twenty-sixth Sunday in Ordinary Time, Year B
First Reading: Numbers 11:25-29

25 The LORD came down in the cloud and spoke to Moses. Taking some of the spirit that was on Moses, the LORD bestowed it on the seventy elders; and as the spirit came to rest on them, they prophesied.

26 Now two men, one named Eldad and the other Medad, were not in the gathering but had been left in the camp. They too had been on the list, but had not gone out to the tent; yet the spirit came to rest on them also, and they prophesied in the camp. 27 So, when a young man quickly told Moses, "Eldad and Medad are prophesying in the camp," 28 Joshua, son of Nun, who from his youth had been Moses' aide, said, "Moses, my lord, stop them." 29 But Moses answered him, "Are you jealous for my sake? Would that all the people of the LORD were prophets! Would that the LORD might bestow his spirit on them all!"

Responsorial Psalm: Psalms 19:8, 10, 12-13, 14
R. (9a) *The precepts of the Lord give joy to the heart.*
8 The law of the LORD is perfect,
     refreshing the soul;
the decree of the LORD is trustworthy,
     giving wisdom to the simple.
R. *The precepts of the Lord give joy to the heart.*

10 The fear of the LORD is pure,
     enduring forever;
the ordinances of the LORD are true,
     all of them just.
R. *The precepts of the Lord give joy to the heart.*

12 Though your servant is careful of them,
     very diligent in keeping them,
13 yet who can detect failings?
     Cleanse me from my unknown faults!
R. *The precepts of the Lord give joy to the heart.*

14 From wanton sin especially, restrain your

servant;
>let it not rule over me.
Then shall I be blameless and innocent
>of serious sin.
R. The precepts of the Lord give joy to the heart.

Second Reading: James 5:1-6

¹ Come now, you rich, weep and wail over your impending miseries. ² Your wealth has rotted away, your clothes have become moth-eaten, ³ your gold and silver have corroded, and that corrosion will be a testimony against you; it will devour your flesh like a fire. You have stored up treasure for the last days. ⁴ Behold, the wages you withheld from the workers who harvested your fields are crying aloud; and the cries of the harvesters have reached the ears of the Lord of hosts. ⁵ You have lived on earth in luxury and pleasure; you have fattened your hearts for the day of slaughter. ⁶ You have condemned; you have murdered the righteous one; he offers you no resistance.

Alleluia: cf. John 17:17B, 17A
R. Alleluia, alleluia.
¹⁷ᴮ Your word, O Lord, is truth;
¹⁷ᴬ consecrate us in the truth.
R. Alleluia, alleluia.

Gospel: Mark 9:38-43, 45, 47-48

³⁸ At that time, John said to Jesus, "Teacher, we saw someone driving out demons in your name, and we tried to prevent him because he does not follow us." ³⁹ Jesus replied, "Do not prevent him. There is no one who performs a mighty deed in my name who can at the same time speak ill of me. ⁴⁰ For whoever is not against us is for us. ⁴¹ Anyone who gives you a cup of water to drink because you belong to Christ, amen, I say to you, will surely not lose his reward.

⁴² "Whoever causes one of these little ones who believe in me to sin, it would be better for him if a great millstone were put around his neck and he were thrown into the sea. ⁴³ If your hand causes you to sin, cut it off. It is better for you to enter into life maimed than with two hands to go into Gehenna, into the unquenchable fire. ⁴⁵ And if your foot causes you to sin, cut if off. It is better for you to enter into life crippled than with two feet to be thrown into Gehenna. ⁴⁷ And if your eye causes you to sin, pluck it out. Better for you to enter into the kingdom of God with one eye than with two eyes to be thrown into Gehenna, ⁴⁸ where 'their worm does not die, and the fire is not quenched.'"

Sunday October 6, 2024

Twenty-seventh Sunday in Ordinary Time, Year B

First Reading: Genesis 2:18-24

[18] The LORD God said: "It is not good for the man to be alone. I will make a suitable partner for him." [19] So the LORD God formed out of the ground various wild animals and various birds of the air, and he brought them to the man to see what he would call them; whatever the man called each of them would be its name. [20] The man gave names to all the cattle, all the birds of the air, and all wild animals; but none proved to be the suitable partner for the man.

[21] So the LORD God cast a deep sleep on the man, and while he was asleep, he took out one of his ribs and closed up its place with flesh. [22] The LORD God then built up into a woman the rib that he had taken from the man. When he brought her to the man, [23] the man said:

"This one, at last, is bone of my bones
    and flesh of my flesh;
this one shall be called 'woman,'
    for out of 'her man' this one has been
        taken."
[24] That is why a man leaves his father and mother and clings to his wife, and the two of them become one flesh.

Responsorial Psalm: Psalms 128:1-2,3,4-5, 6

R. (cf. 5) *May the Lord bless us all the days of our lives.*

[1] Blessed are you who fear the LORD,
        who walk in his ways!
[2] For you shall eat the fruit of your
        handiwork;
    blessed shall you be, and favored.
R. *May the Lord bless us all the days of our lives.*

[3] Your wife shall be like a fruitful vine
        in the recesses of your home,
your children like olive plants
        around your table.
R. *May the Lord bless us all the days of our lives.*

[4] Behold, thus is the man blessed
        who fears the LORD.
[5] The LORD bless you from Zion:

may you see the prosperity of Jerusalem
all the days of your life.
R. May the Lord bless us all the days of our lives.

⁶ May you see your children's children.
Peace be upon Israel!
R. May the Lord bless us all the days of our lives.

Second Reading: Hebrews 2:9-11

Brothers and sisters: ⁹ He "for a little while" was made "lower than the angels," that by the grace of God he might taste death for everyone.

¹⁰ For it was fitting that he, for whom and through whom all things exist, in bringing many children to glory, should make the leader to their salvation perfect through suffering. ¹¹ He who consecrates and those who are being consecrated all have one origin. Therefore, he is not ashamed to call them "brothers."

Alleluia: 1 John 4:12

R. Alleluia, alleluia.

¹² If we love one another, God remains in us
and his love is brought to perfection in us.

R. Alleluia, alleluia.

Gospel: Mark 10:2-16

² The Pharisees approached Jesus and asked, "Is it lawful for a husband to divorce his wife?" They were testing him. ³ He said to them in reply, "What did Moses command you?" ⁴ They replied, "Moses permitted a husband to write a bill of divorce and dismiss her." ⁵ But Jesus told them, "Because of the hardness of your hearts he wrote you this commandment. ⁶ But from the beginning of creation, *God made them male and female.* ⁷ *For this reason a man shall leave his father and mother and be joined to his wife,* ⁸ *and the two shall become one flesh.* So they are no longer two but one flesh. ⁹ Therefore what God has joined together, no human being must separate." ¹⁰ In the house the disciples again questioned Jesus about this. ¹¹ He said to them, "Whoever divorces his wife and marries another commits adultery against her; ¹² and if she divorces her husband and marries another, she commits adultery."

¹³ And people were bringing children to him that he might touch them, but the disciples rebuked them. ¹⁴ When Jesus saw this he became indignant and said to them, "Let the children come to me; do not prevent them, for the kingdom of God belongs to such as these. ¹⁵ Amen, I say to you, whoever does not accept the

kingdom of God like a child will not enter it." [16] Then he embraced them and blessed them, placing his hands on them.

Or Mark 10:2-12

[2] The Pharisees approached Jesus and asked, "Is it lawful for a husband to divorce his wife?" They were testing him. [3] He said to them in reply, "What did Moses command you?" [4] They replied, "Moses permitted a husband to write a bill of divorce and dismiss her." [5] But Jesus told them, "Because of the hardness of your hearts he wrote you this commandment. [6] But from the beginning of creation, *God made them male and female. [7]For this reason a man shall leave his father and mother and be joined to his wife, [8] and the two shall become one flesh*. So they are no longer two but one flesh. [9] Therefore what God has joined together, no human being must separate." [10] In the house the disciples again questioned Jesus about this. [11] He said to them, "Whoever divorces his wife and marries another commits adultery against her; [12] and if she divorces her husband and marries another, she commits adultery."

Sunday October 13, 2024
Twenty-eighth Sunday in Ordinary Time, Year B
First Reading: Wisdom 7:7-11

[7] I prayed, and prudence was given me;
    I pleaded, and the spirit of wisdom came
       to me.
[8] I preferred her to scepter and throne,
and deemed riches nothing in comparison
       with her,
    [9] nor did I liken any priceless gem to her;
because all gold, in view of her, is a little
       sand,
    and before her, silver is to be accounted
       mire.
[10] Beyond health and comeliness I loved her,
and I chose to have her rather than the light,
    because the splendor of her never yields
       to sleep.
[11] Yet all good things together came to me in
       her company,
    and countless riches at her hands.

Responsorial Psalm: Psalms 90:12-13, 14-15, 16-17

R. [14] *Fill us with your love, O Lord, and we will*
sing for joy!

[12] Teach us to number our days aright,
    that we may gain wisdom of heart.
[13] Return, O LORD! How long?
    Have pity on your servants!

R. Fill us with your love, O Lord, and we will
sing for joy!

[14] Fill us at daybreak with your kindness,
    that we may shout for joy and gladness
        all our days.
[15] Make us glad, for the days when you afflicted
        us,
    for the years when we saw evil.

R. Fill us with your love, O Lord, and we will
sing for joy!

[16] Let your work be seen by your servants
    and your glory by their children;
[17] and may the gracious care of the LORD our
        God be ours;
    prosper the work of our hands for us!
    Prosper the work of our hands!

R. Fill us with your love, O Lord, and we will
sing for joy!

Second Reading: Hebrews 4:12-13

Brothers and sisters: [12] Indeed the word of God is living and effective, sharper than any two-edged sword, penetrating even between soul and spirit, joints and marrow, and able to discern reflections and thoughts of the heart. [13] No creature is concealed from him, but everything is naked and exposed to the eyes of him to whom we must render an account.

Alleluia: Matthew 5:3

R. Alleluia, alleluia.
[3] Blessed are the poor in spirit,
for theirs is the kingdom of heaven.

R. Alleluia, alleluia.

Gospel: Mark 10:17-30

[17] As Jesus was setting out on a journey, a man ran up, knelt down before him, and asked him, "Good teacher, what must I do to inherit eternal life?" [18] Jesus answered him, "Why do you call me good? No one is good but God alone. [19] You know the commandments: *You shall not kill; you shall not commit adultery; you shall not steal; you shall not bear false witness; you shall not defraud; honor your father and your mother.*" [20] He replied and said to him, "Teacher, all of these I have observed from my youth." [21] Jesus, looking at him, loved him and said to him, "You are lacking in one thing. Go, sell what you have, and give to the poor and you will have treasure in heaven; then come, follow me." [22] At that statement his face fell, and he went away sad, for he had many possessions.

[23] Jesus looked around and said to his disciples, "How hard it is for those who have wealth to enter the kingdom of God!" [24] The disciples were amazed at his words. So Jesus again said to them in reply, "Children, how hard it is to enter the kingdom of God! [25] It is easier for a camel to pass through the eye of a needle than for one who is rich to enter the kingdom of God." [26] They were exceedingly astonished and said among themselves, "Then who can be saved?" [27] Jesus looked at them and said, "For human beings it is impossible, but not for God. All things are possible for God." [28] Peter began to say to him, "We have given up everything and followed you." [29] Jesus said, "Amen, I say to you, there is no one who has given up house or brothers or sisters or mother or father or children or lands for my sake and for the sake of the gospel [30] who will not receive a hundred times more now in this present age: houses and brothers and sisters and mothers and children and lands, with persecutions, and eternal life in the age to come."

Or Mark 10:17-27

[17] As Jesus was setting out on a journey, a man ran up, knelt down before him, and asked him, "Good teacher, what must I do to inherit eternal life?" [18] Jesus answered him, "Why do you call me good? No one is good but God alone. [19] You know the commandments: *You shall not kill; you shall not commit adultery; you shall not steal; you shall not bear false witness; you shall not defraud; honor your father and your mother.*" [20] He replied and said to him, "Teacher, all of these I have observed from my youth." [21] Jesus, looking at him, loved him and said to him, "You are lacking in one thing. Go, sell what you have, and give to the poor and you will have treasure in heaven; then come, follow me." [22] At that statement his face fell, and he went away sad, for he had many possessions.

²³ Jesus looked around and said to his disciples, "How hard it is for those who have wealth to enter the kingdom of God!" ²⁴ The disciples were amazed at his words. So Jesus again said to them in reply, "Children, how hard it is to enter the kingdom of God! ²⁵ It is easier for a camel to pass through the eye of a needle than for one who is rich to enter the kingdom of God." ²⁶ They were exceedingly astonished and said among themselves, "Then who can be saved?" ²⁷ Jesus looked at them and said, "For human beings it is impossible, but not for God. All things are possible for God."

Sunday October 20, 2024
Twenty-ninth Week Sunday in Ordinary Time, Year B

First Reading: Isaiah 53:10-11

¹⁰ The LORD was pleased
   to crush him in infirmity.

If he gives his life as an offering for sin,
   he shall see his descendants in a long life,
   and the will of the LORD shall be
      accomplished through him.

¹¹ Because of his affliction
   he shall see the light in fullness of days;
through his suffering, my servant shall
      justify many,
   and their guilt he shall bear.

Responsorial Psalm: Psalms 33:4-5, 18-19, 20, 22

R. ⁽²²⁾ *Lord, let your mercy be on us, as we place*
                  our trust in you.

⁴ Upright is the word of the LORD,
      and all his works are trustworthy.
⁵ He loves justice and right;
      of the kindness of the LORD the earth is
      full.

R. Lord, let your mercy be on us, as we place our
                  trust in you.

¹⁸ See, the eyes of the LORD are upon those who
      fear him,
      upon those who hope for his kindness,

¹⁹ To deliver them from death
> and preserve them in spite of famine.
R. Lord, let your mercy be on us, as we place our
> **trust in you.**

²⁰ Our soul waits for the LORD,
> who is our help and our shield.
²² May your kindness, O LORD, be upon us
> who have put our hope in you.
R. Lord, let your mercy be on us, as we place our
> **trust in you.**

Second Reading: Hebrews 4:14-16

Brothers and sisters: ¹⁴ Since we have a great high priest who has passed through the heavens, Jesus, the Son of God, let us hold fast to our confession. ¹⁵ For we do not have a high priest who is unable to sympathize with our weaknesses, but one who has similarly been tested in every way, yet without sin. ¹⁶ So let us confidently approach the throne of grace to receive mercy and to find grace for timely help.

Alleluia: Mark 10:45

R. Alleluia, alleluia.
⁴⁵ The Son of Man came to serve
and to give his life as a ransom for many.
R. Alleluia, alleluia.

Gospel: Mark 10:35-45

³⁵ James and John, the sons of Zebedee, came to Jesus and said to him, "Teacher, we want you to do for us whatever we ask of you." ³⁶ He replied, "What do you wish me to do for you?" ³⁷ They answered him, "Grant that in your glory we may sit one at your right and the other at your left." ³⁸ Jesus said to them, "You do not know what you are asking. Can you drink the cup that I drink or be baptized with the baptism with which I am baptized?" ³⁹ They said to him, "We can." Jesus said to them, "The cup that I drink, you will drink, and with the baptism with which I am baptized, you will be baptized; ⁴⁰ but to sit at my right or at my left is not mine to give but is for those for whom it has been prepared." ⁴¹ When the ten heard this, they became indignant at James and John. ⁴² Jesus summoned them and said to them, "You know that those who are recognized as rulers over the Gentiles lord it over them, and their great ones make their authority over them felt. ⁴³ But it shall not be so among you. Rather, whoever wishes to be great among you will be your servant; ⁴⁴ whoever wishes to be first among you will be the

slave of all. [45] For the Son of Man did not come to be served but to serve and to give his life as a ransom for many."

Or Mark 10:42-45

[42] Jesus summoned the Twelve and said to them, "You know that those who are recognized as rulers over the Gentiles lord it over them, and their great ones make their authority over them felt. [43] But it shall not be so among you. Rather, whoever wishes to be great among you will be your servant; [44] whoever wishes to be first among you will be the slave of all. [45] For the Son of Man did not come to be served but to serve and to give his life as a ransom for many."

Sunday October 27, 2024
Thirtieth Sunday in Ordinary Time, Year B

First Reading: Jeremiah 31:7-9

[7] Thus says the LORD:

Shout with joy for Jacob,
　　exult at the head of the nations;
　　proclaim your praise and say:
The LORD has delivered his people,
　　the remnant of Israel.
[8] Behold, I will bring them back
　　from the land of the north;
I will gather them from the ends of the
　　　　world,
　　with the blind and the lame in their
　　　　midst,
the mothers and those with child;
　　they shall return as an immense throng.
[9] They departed in tears,
　　but I will console them and guide them;
I will lead them to brooks of water,
　　on a level road, so that none shall
　　　　stumble.
For I am a father to Israel,
　　Ephraim is my first-born.

Responsorial Psalm: Psalms 126:1-2, 2-3, 4-5, 6
R. *(3) The Lord has done great things for us; we*

are filled with joy.

[1] When the LORD brought back the captives of
    Zion,
    we were like men dreaming.
[2AB] Then our mouth was filled with laughter,
    and our tongue with rejoicing.

R. The Lord has done great things for us; we are
    filled with joy.

[2BC] Then they said among the nations,
    "The LORD has done great things for
    them."
[3] The LORD has done great things for us;
    we are glad indeed.

R. The Lord has done great things for us; we are
    filled with joy.

[4] Restore our fortunes, O LORD,
    like the torrents in the southern desert.
[5] Those that sow in tears
    shall reap rejoicing.

R. The Lord has done great things for us; we are
    filled with joy.

[6] Although they go forth weeping,
    carrying the seed to be sown,
They shall come back rejoicing,
    carrying their sheaves.

R. The Lord has done great things for us; we are
    filled with joy.

Second Reading: Hebrews 5:1-6

Brothers and sisters: [1] Every high priest is taken from among men and made their representative before God, to offer gifts and sacrifices for sins. [2] He is able to deal patiently with the ignorant and erring, for he himself is beset by weakness [3] and so, for this reason, must make sin offerings for himself as well as for the people. [4] No one takes this honor upon himself but only when called by God, just as Aaron was. [5] In the same way, it was not Christ who glorified himself in becoming high priest, but rather the one who said to him:

You are my son: this day I have begotten you;

⁶ just as he says in another place:

*You are a priest forever according to the
        order of Melchizedek.*

Alleluia: cf. 2 Timothy 1:10
R. Alleluia, alleluia.
¹⁰ Our Savior Jesus Christ destroyed death
and brought life to light through the Gospel.
R. Alleluia, alleluia.

Gospel: Mark 10:46-52
⁴⁶ As Jesus was leaving Jericho with his disciples and a sizable crowd, Bartimaeus, a blind man, the son of Timaeus, sat by the roadside begging. ⁴⁷ On hearing that it was Jesus of Nazareth, he began to cry out and say, "Jesus, son of David, have pity on me." ⁴⁸ And many rebuked him, telling him to be silent. But he kept calling out all the more, "Son of David, have pity on me." ⁴⁹ Jesus stopped and said, "Call him." So they called the blind man, saying to him, "Take courage; get up, Jesus is calling you." ⁵⁰ He threw aside his cloak, sprang up, and came to Jesus. ⁵¹ Jesus said to him in reply, "What do you want me to do for you?" The blind man replied to him, "Master, I want to see." ⁵² Jesus told him, "Go your way; your faith has saved you." Immediately he received his sight and followed him on the way.

Sunday November 3, 2024
Thirty-first Sunday in Ordinary Time, Year B
First Reading: Deuteronomy 6:2-6
Moses spoke to the people, saying: ² "Fear the LORD, your God, and keep, throughout the days of your lives, all his statutes and commandments which I enjoin on you, and thus have long life. ³ Hear then, Israel, and be careful to observe them, that you may grow and prosper the more, in keeping with the promise of the LORD, the God of your fathers, to give you a land flowing with milk and honey.

⁴ "Hear, O Israel! The LORD is our God, the LORD alone! ⁵ Therefore, you shall love the LORD, your God, with all your heart, and with all your soul, and with all your strength. ⁶ Take to heart these words which I enjoin on you today."

Responsorial Psalm: Psalms 18:2-3, 3-4, 47, 51

R. *(2) I love you, Lord, my strength.*

² I love you, O LORD, my strength,
    ³ᴬ O LORD, my rock, my fortress, my
        deliverer.
R. *I love you, Lord, my strength.*

³ᴮ My God, my rock of refuge,
    my shield, the horn of my salvation, my
        stronghold!
⁴ Praised be the LORD, I exclaim,
    and I am safe from my enemies.
R. *I love you, Lord, my strength.*

⁴⁷ The LORD lives! And blessed be my rock!
    Extolled be God my savior.
⁵¹ You who gave great victories to your king
    and showed kindness to your anointed.
R. *I love you, Lord, my strength.*

Second Reading: Hebrews 7:23-28

Brothers and sisters: ²³ The levitical priests were many because they were prevented by death from remaining in office, ²⁴ but Jesus, because he remains forever, has a priesthood that does not pass away. ²⁵ Therefore, he is always able to save those who approach God through him, since he lives forever to make intercession for them.

²⁶ It was fitting that we should have such a high priest: holy, innocent, undefiled, separated from sinners, higher than the heavens. ²⁷ He has no need, as did the high priests, to offer sacrifice day after day, first for his own sins and then for those of the people; he did that once for all when he offered himself. ²⁸ For the law appoints men subject to weakness to be high priests, but the word of the oath, which was taken after the law, appoints a son, who has been made perfect forever.

Alleluia: John 14:23

R. Alleluia, alleluia.
²³ Whoever loves me will keep my word,
says the Lord; and my Father will love him
and we will come to him.
R. Alleluia, alleluia.

Gospel: Mark 12:28B-34

28B One of the scribes came to Jesus and asked him, "Which is the first of all the commandments?" 29 Jesus replied, "The first is this: *Hear, O Israel! The Lord our God is Lord alone!* 30 *You shall love the Lord your God with all your heart, with all your soul, with all your mind, and with all your strength.* 31 The second is this: *You shall love your neighbor as yourself.* There is no other commandment greater than these." 32 The scribe said to him, "Well said, teacher. You are right in saying, 'He is One and there is no other than he.' 33 And 'to love him with all your heart, with all your understanding, with all your strength, and to love your neighbor as yourself' is worth more than all burnt offerings and sacrifices." 34 And when Jesus saw that he answered with understanding, he said to him, "You are not far from the kingdom of God." And no one dared to ask him any more questions.

Sunday November 10, 2024
Thirty-second Sunday in ordinary Time, Year B
First Reading: 1 Kings 17:10-16

10 In those days, Elijah the prophet went to Zarephath. As he arrived at the entrance of the city, a widow was gathering sticks there; he called out to her, "Please bring me a small cupful of water to drink." 11 She left to get it, and he called out after her, "Please bring along a bit of bread." 12 She answered, "As the LORD, your God, lives, I have nothing baked; there is only a handful of flour in my jar and a little oil in my jug. Just now I was collecting a couple of sticks, to go in and prepare something for myself and my son; when we have eaten it, we shall die." 13 Elijah said to her, "Do not be afraid. Go and do as you propose. But first make me a little cake and bring it to me. Then you can prepare something for yourself and your son. 14 For the LORD, the God of Israel, says, 'The jar of flour shall not go empty, nor the jug of oil run dry, until the day when the LORD sends rain upon the earth.'" 15 She left and did as Elijah had said. She was able to eat for a year, and he and her son as well; 16 the jar of flour did not go empty, nor the jug of oil run dry, as the LORD had foretold through Elijah.

Responsorial Psalm: Psalms 146:7, 8-9, 9-10
R. (1b) *Praise the Lord, my soul!* or: *Alleluia.*
7 The LORD keeps faith forever,
    secures justice for the oppressed,
    gives food to the hungry.
The LORD sets captives free.
R. *Praise the Lord, my soul!* or: *Alleluia.*

⁸ The LORD gives sight to the blind;
>   the LORD raises up those who were bowed
>   down.
> The LORD loves the just;
>   ^{9A} the LORD protects strangers.

R. Praise the Lord, my soul! or: **Alleluia.**

^{9B} The fatherless and the widow he sustains,
>   but the way of the wicked he thwarts.
> ¹⁰ The LORD shall reign forever;
>   your God, O Zion, through all generations.
>   Alleluia.

R. Praise the Lord, my soul! or: **Alleluia.**

Second Reading: Hebrews 9:24-28

²⁴ Christ did not enter into a sanctuary made by hands, a copy of the true one, but heaven itself, that he might now appear before God on our behalf. ²⁵ Not that he might offer himself repeatedly, as the high priest enters each year into the sanctuary with blood that is not his own; ²⁶ if that were so, he would have had to suffer repeatedly from the foundation of the world. But now once for all he has appeared at the end of the ages to take away sin by his sacrifice. ²⁷ Just as it is appointed that human beings die once, and after this the judgment, ²⁸ so also Christ, offered once to take away the sins of many, will appear a second time, not to take away sin but to bring salvation to those who eagerly await him.

Alleluia: Mark 5:3

R. Alleluia, alleluia.
³ Blessed are the poor in spirit,
for theirs is the kingdom of heaven.
R. Alleluia, alleluia.

Gospel: Mark 12:38-44

³⁸ In the course of his teaching Jesus said to the crowds, "Beware of the scribes, who like to go around in long robes and accept greetings in the marketplaces, ³⁹ seats of honor in synagogues, and places of honor at banquets. ⁴⁰ They devour the houses of widows and, as a pretext, recite lengthy prayers. They will receive a very severe condemnation."

[41] He sat down opposite the treasury and observed how the crowd put money into the treasury. Many rich people put in large sums. [42] A poor widow also came and put in two small coins worth a few cents. [43] Calling his disciples to himself, he said to them, "Amen, I say to you, this poor widow put in more than all the other contributors to the treasury. [44] For they have all contributed from their surplus wealth, but she, from her poverty, has contributed all she had, her whole livelihood."

Or Mark 12:41-44

[41] Jesus sat down opposite the treasury and observed how the crowd put money into the treasury. Many rich people put in large sums. [42] A poor widow also came and put in two small coins worth a few cents. [43] Calling his disciples to himself, he said to them, "Amen, I say to you, this poor widow put in more than all the other contributors to the treasury. [44] For they have all contributed from their surplus wealth, but she, from her poverty, has contributed all she had, her whole livelihood."

Sunday November 17, 2024
Thirty-third Sunday in Ordinary Time, Year B
First Reading: Daniel 12:1-3

[1] In those days, I Daniel, heard this word of the Lord:

"At that time there shall arise
    Michael, the great prince,
    guardian of your people;
it shall be a time unsurpassed in distress
    since nations began until that time.
At that time your people shall escape,
    everyone who is found written in the
        book.

[2] "Many of those who sleep in the dust of the
        earth shall awake;
    some shall live forever,
    others shall be an everlasting horror and
        disgrace.

[3] "But the wise shall shine brightly
    like the splendor of the firmament,
and those who lead the many to justice

shall be like the stars forever."

Responsorial Psalm: Psalms 16:5, 8,9-10, 11
R. *(1) You are my inheritance, O Lord!*
[5] O LORD, my allotted portion and my cup,
    you it is who hold fast my lot.
[8] I set the LORD ever before me;
    with him at my right hand I shall not be
        disturbed.
R. *You are my inheritance, O Lord!*

[9] Therefore my heart is glad and my soul
        rejoices,
    my body, too, abides in confidence;
[10] because you will not abandon my soul to the
        netherworld,
    nor will you suffer your faithful one to
        undergo corruption.
R. *You are my inheritance, O Lord!*

[11] You will show me the path to life,
    fullness of joys in your presence,
    the delights at your right hand forever.
R. *You are my inheritance, O Lord!*

Second Reading: Hebrews 10:11-14, 18
Brothers and sisters: [11] Every priest stands daily at his ministry, offering frequently those same sacrifices that can never take away sins. [12] But this one offered one sacrifice for sins, and took his seat forever at the right hand of God; [13] now he waits until his enemies are made his footstool. [14] For by one offering he has made perfect forever those who are being consecrated.

    [18] Where there is forgiveness of these, there is no longer offering for sin.

Alleluia: Luke 21:36
R. Alleluia, alleluia.
[36] Be vigilant at all times
and pray that you have the strength to stand
    before the Son of Man.
R. Alleluia, alleluia.

Gospel: Mark 13:24-32

Jesus said to his disciples: [24] "In those days after that tribulation
the sun will be darkened,
   and the moon will not give its light,
[25] and the stars will be falling from the sky,
   and the powers in the heavens will be
      shaken.

[26] "And then they will see 'the Son of Man coming in the clouds' with great power and glory, [27] and then he will send out the angels and gather his elect from the four winds, from the end of the earth to the end of the sky.

[28] "Learn a lesson from the fig tree. When its branch becomes tender and sprouts leaves, you know that summer is near. [29] In the same way, when you see these things happening, know that he is near, at the gates. [30] Amen, I say to you, this generation will not pass away until all these things have taken place. [31] Heaven and earth will pass away, but my words will not pass away.

[32] "But of that day or hour, no one knows, neither the angels in heaven, nor the Son, but only the Father."

Sunday November 24, 2024
Feast of Christ the Universal King, Year B

First Reading: Daniel 7:13-14

[13] As the visions during the night continued, I saw

one like a Son of man coming,
   on the clouds of heaven;
when he reached the Ancient One
   and was presented before him,
[14] the one like a Son of man received dominion,
      glory, and kingship;
   all peoples, nations, and languages serve
      him.
His dominion is an everlasting dominion
   that shall not be taken away,
   his kingship shall not be destroyed.

Responsorial Psalm: Psalms 93:1, 1-2, 5
R. [1a] *The Lord is king; he is robed in majesty.*

¹ᴬᴮ The LORD is king, in splendor robed;
    robed is the LORD and girt about with
        strength.
R. The Lord is king; he is robed in majesty.

¹ᶜ And he has made the world firm,
    not to be moved.
² Your throne stands firm from of old;
    from everlasting you are, O LORD.
R. The Lord is king; he is robed in majesty.

⁵ Your decrees are worthy of trust indeed;
    holiness befits your house,
        O LORD, for length of days.
R. The Lord is king; he is robed in majesty.

Second Reading: Revelation 1:5-8

⁵ Jesus Christ is the faithful witness, the firstborn of the dead and ruler of the kings of the earth. To him who loves us and has freed us from our sins by his blood, ⁶ who has made us into a kingdom, priests for his God and Father, to him be glory and power forever and ever. Amen.

⁷ Behold, he is coming amid the clouds,
    and every eye will see him,
        even those who pierced him.
All the peoples of the earth will lament him.
    Yes. Amen.
⁸ "I am the Alpha and the Omega, " says the Lord God, "the one who is and who was and who is to come, the almighty."

Alleluia: Mark 11:9, 10
R. Alleluia, alleluia.
⁹ Blessed is he who comes in the name of the
        Lord!
¹⁰ Blessed is the kingdom of our father David
        that is to come!
R. Alleluia, alleluia.

Gospel: John 18:33B-37

³³ᴮ Pilate said to Jesus, "Are you the King of the Jews?" ³⁴ Jesus answered, "Do you say this on your own or have others told you about me?" ³⁵ Pilate answered, "I am not a Jew, am I? Your own nation and the chief priests handed you over to me. What have you done?" ³⁶ Jesus answered, "My kingdom does not belong to this world. If my kingdom did belong to this world, my attendants would be fighting to keep me from being handed over to the Jews. But as it is, my kingdom is not here." ³⁷ So Pilate said to him, "Then you are a king?" Jesus answered, "You say I am a king. For this I was born and for this I came into the world, to testify to the truth. Everyone who belongs to the truth listens to my voice."

Sunday December 1, 2024
First Sunday of Advent, Year C

First Reading: Jeremiah 33:14-16

¹⁴ The days are coming, says the LORD,
    when I will fulfill the promise
    I made to the house of Israel and Judah.
¹⁵ In those days, at that time,
    I will raise up for David a just shoot;
    he shall do what is right and just in the
        land.
¹⁶ In those days Judah shall be safe
    and Jerusalem shall dwell secure;
    this is the name they shall call her:
    "The LORD our justice."

Responsorial Psalm: Psalms 25:4-5, 8-9, 10, 14
R. ⁽¹ᵇ⁾ *To you, O Lord, I lift my soul.*
⁴ Yours ways, O LORD, make known to me;
    teach me your paths.
⁵ guide me in your truth and teach me,
    for you are God my savior,
    and for you I wait all the day.
R. *To you, O Lord, I lift my soul.*

⁸ Good and upright is the LORD,
    thus he shows sinners the way,
⁹ He guides the humble in justice,
    and teaches the humble his way.

R. To you, O Lord, I lift my soul.

¹⁰ All the paths of the Lord are kindness and
    constancy
  toward those who keep his covenant and
    his decrees.
¹⁴ The friendship of the LORD is with those who
    fear him;
  and his covenant, for their instruction.
R. To you, O Lord, I lift my soul.

Second Reading: 1 Thessalonians 3:12-4:2

Brothers and sisters, ¹² May the Lord make you increase and abound in love for one another and for all, just as we have for you, ¹³ so as to strengthen your hearts, to be blameless in holiness before our God and Father at the coming of our Lord Jesus with all his holy ones. Amen.

¹ Finally, brothers and sisters, we earnestly ask and exhort you in the Lord Jesus that, as you received from us how you should conduct yourselves to please God—and as you are conducting yourselves—you do so even more. ² For you know what instructions we gave you through the Lord Jesus.

Alleluia: Psalms 85:8

R. Alleluia, alleluia.
⁸ Show us, Lord, your love;
and grant us your salvation.
R. Alleluia, alleluia.

Gospel: Luke 21:25-28, 34-36

Jesus said to his disciples: ²⁵ "There will be signs in the sun, the moon, and the stars, and on earth nations will be in dismay, perplexed by the roaring of the sea and the waves. ²⁶ People will die of fright in anticipation of what is coming upon the world, for the powers of the heavens will be shaken. ²⁷ And then they will see the Son of Man coming in a cloud with power and great glory. ²⁸ But when these signs begin to happen, stand erect and raise your heads because your redemption is at hand."

³⁴ "Beware that your hearts do not become drowsy from carousing and drunkenness and the anxieties of daily life, and that day catch you by surprise ³⁵ like a trap. For that day will assault everyone who lives on the face of the earth. ³⁶ Be vigilant at all times and pray that you have the strength to escape the tribulations that are imminent and to stand before the Son of Man."

Second Sunday of Advent, Year C

First Reading: Baruch 5:1-9

[1] Jerusalem, take off your robe of mourning
      and misery;
  put on the splendor of glory from God
      forever:
[2] Wrapped in the mantle of justice from God,
   bear on your head the mitre
   that displays the glory of the eternal
      name.
[3] For God will show all the earth your
      splendor:
   [4] you will be named by God forever
   the peace of justice, the glory of God's worship.
[5] Up, Jerusalem! stand upon the heights;
   look to the east and see your children
gathered from the east and the west
   at the word of the Holy One,
   rejoicing that they are remembered by
      God.
[6] Led away on foot by their enemies they left
      you:
   but God will bring them back to you
   borne aloft in glory as on royal thrones.
[7] For God has commanded
   that every lofty mountain be made low,
   and the age-old depths and gorges,
   be filled to level ground,
   that Israel may advance secure in the
      glory of God.
[8] The forests and every kind of fragrant tree
   have overshadowed Israel at God's
      command;
[9] for God is leading Israel in joy
   by the light of his glory,
   with the mercy and justice for company.

Responsorial Psalm: Psalms 126:1-2, 2-3, 4-5, 6

R. *(3)* *The Lord has done great things for us; we*
         are filled with joy.

[1] When the LORD brought back the captives of
         Zion,
   we thought we were dreaming.
[2AB] Then our mouths were filled with laughter;
   and our tongue with rejoicing.
[2BC] Then they said among the nations,
   "The LORD had done great things for
them."
[3] The Lord has done great things for us;
   we are glad indeed.

R. *The Lord has done great things for us; we are*
         filled with joy.

[4] Restore our fortunes, O LORD,
   like the torrents in the southern desert.
[5] Those who sow in tears
   shall reap rejoicing.

R. *The Lord has done great things for us; we are*
         filled with joy.

[6] Although they go forth weeping,
   carrying the seed to be sown,
they shall some back rejoicing,
   carrying their sheaves.

R. *The Lord has done great things for us; we are*
         filled with joy.

Second Reading: Philippians 1:4-6, 8-11

Brothers and sisters: [4] I pray always with joy in my every prayer for all of you, [5] because of your partnership for the gospel from the first day until now. [6] I am confident of this, that the one who began a good work in you will continue to complete it until the day of Christ Jesus. [8] For God is my witness, how I long for all of you with the affection of Christ Jesus. [9] And this is my prayer: that your love may increase ever more and more in knowledge and every kind of perception, [10] to discern what is of value, so that you may be pure and blameless for the day of Christ, [11] filled with the fruit of righteousness that comes through Jesus Christ for the glory and praise of God.

Alleluia: Luke 3:4, 6
R. Alleluia, alleluia.
[4] Prepare the way of the Lord, make straight
      his paths:
[6] all flesh shall see the salvation of God.
R. Alleluia, alleluia.

Gospel: Luke 3:1-6
[1] In the fifteenth year of the reign of Tiberius Caesar, when Pontius Pilate was governor of Judea, and Herod was tetrarch of Galilee, and his brother Philip tetrarch of the region of Ituraea and Trachonitis, and Lysanias was tetrarch of Abilene, [2] during the high priesthood of Annas and Caiaphas, the word of God came to John the son of Zechariah in the desert. [3] He went throughout the whole region of the Jordan, proclaiming a baptism of repentance for the forgiveness of sins, [4] as it is written in the book of the words of the prophet Isaiah:

"A voice of one crying out in the desert:
'Prepare the way of the Lord,
*   make straight his paths.*
[5] *Every valley shall be filled*
*   and every mountain and hill shall be made low.*
The winding roads shall be made straight,
*   and the rough ways made smooth,*
[6] *and all flesh shall see the salvation of God.'"*

Sunday December 15, 2024
Third Sunday of Advent, Year C

First Reading: Zephaniah 3:14-18A
[14] Shout for joy, O daughter Zion!
      Sing joyfully, O Israel!
Be glad and exult with all your heart,
      O daughter Jerusalem!
[15] The LORD has removed the judgment against
            you
      he has turned away your enemies;
the King of Israel, the LORD, is in your midst,

you have no further misfortune to fear.
16 On that day, it shall be said to Jerusalem:
Fear not, O Zion, be not discouraged!
17 The LORD, your God, is in your midst,
a mighty savior;
he will rejoice over you with gladness,
and renew you in his love,
he will sing joyfully because of you,
18A as one sings at festivals.

Responsorial Psalm: Isaiah 12:2-3, 4, 5-6.

R. (6) *Cry out with joy and gladness: for among*
you is the great and Holy One of Israel.
2 God indeed is my savior;
I am confident and unafraid.
My strength and my courage is the LORD,
and he has been my savior.
3 With joy you will draw water
at the fountain of salvation.
R. *Cry out with joy and gladness: for among you*
is the great and Holy One of Israel.

4 Give thanks to the LORD, acclaim his name;
among the nations make known his
deeds,
proclaim how exalted is his name.
R. *Cry out with joy and gladness: for among you*
is the great and Holy One of Israel.

5 Sing praise to the LORD for his glorious
achievement;
let this be known throughout all the
earth.
6 Shout with exultation, O city of Zion,
for great in your midst
is the Holy One of Israel!
R. *Cry out with joy and gladness: for among you*
is the great and Holy One of Israel.

Second Reading: Philippians 4:4-7

Brothers and sisters: [4] Rejoice in the Lord always. I shall say it again: rejoice! [5] Your kindness should be known to all. The Lord is near. [6] Have no anxiety at all, but in everything, by prayer and petition, with thanksgiving, make your requests known to God. [7]Then the peace of God that surpasses all understanding will guard your hearts and minds in Christ Jesus.

Alleluia: Isaiah 61:1 (Cited In Luke 4:18)

R. Alleluia, alleluia.

[1] The Spirit of the Lord is upon me,
because he has anointed me
to bring glad tidings to the poor.

R. Alleluia, alleluia.

Gospel: Luke 3:10-18

[10] The crowds asked John the Baptist, "What should we do?" [11] He said to them in reply, "Whoever has two cloaks should share with the person who has none. And whoever has food should do likewise." [12] Even tax collectors came to be baptized and they said to him, "Teacher, what should we do?" [13]He answered them, "Stop collecting more than what is prescribed." [14] Soldiers also asked him, "And what is it that we should do?" He told them, "Do not practice extortion, do not falsely accuse anyone, and be satisfied with your wages."

[15] Now the people were filled with expectation, and all were asking in their hearts whether John might be the Christ. [16] John answered them all, saying, "I am baptizing you with water, but one mightier than I is coming. I am not worthy to loosen the thongs of his sandals. He will baptize you with the Holy Spirit and fire. [17] His winnowing fan is in his hand to clear his threshing floor and to gather the wheat into his barn, but the chaff he will burn with unquenchable fire." [18] Exhorting them in many other ways, he preached good news to the people.

Sunday December 22, 2024
Fourth Sunday of Advent, Year C

First Reading: Micah 5:1-4A

Thus says the LORD:

[1] You, Bethlehem-Ephrathah,
    too small to be among the clans of Judah,
from you shall come forth for me

one who is to be ruler in Israel;
whose origin is from of old,
    from ancient times.
    [2] Therefore the Lord will give them up,
        until the time
    when she who is to give birth has borne,
and the rest of his kindred shall return
    to the children of Israel.
[3] He shall stand firm and shepherd his flock
    by the strength of the LORD,
    in the majestic name of the LORD, his God;
and they shall remain, for now his greatness
    shall reach to the ends of the earth;
    [4A] he shall be peace.

Responsorial Psalm: Psalms 80:2-3, 15-16, 18-19.
R. [(4)] Lord, make us turn to you; let us see your
*   face and we shall be saved.*
[2] O shepherd of Israel, hearken,
    from your throne upon the cherubim,
        shine forth.
[3] Rouse your power,
    and come to save us.
R. Lord, make us turn to you; let us see your face
*   and we shall be saved.*

[15] Once again, O LORD of hosts,
    look down from heaven, and see;
take care of this vine,
    [16] and protect what your right hand has
        planted
    the son of man whom you yourself made
        strong.
R. Lord, make us turn to you; let us see your face
*   and we shall be saved.*

[18] May your help be with the man of your right
        hand,
    with the son of man whom you yourself made

strong.

^{19} Then we will no more withdraw from you;
    give us new life, and we will call upon
        your name.

***R. Lord, make us turn to you; let us see your face
        and we shall be saved.***

Second Reading: Hebrews 10:5-10

Brothers and sisters: ^{5} When Christ came into the world, he said:

"Sacrifice and offering you did not desire,
    but a body you prepared for me;
        ^{6} in holocausts and sin offerings you took
            no delight.
^{7} Then I said, 'As is written of me in the scroll,
    behold, I come to do your will, O God.'"

^{8} First he says, "Sacrifices and offerings, holocausts and sin offerings, you neither desired nor delighted in." These are offered according to the law. ^{9} Then he says, "Behold, I come to do your will." He takes away the first to establish the second. ^{10} By this "will," we have been consecrated through the offering of the body of Jesus Christ once for all.

Alleluia: Luke 1:38
R. Alleluia, alleluia.
^{38} Behold, I am the handmaid of the Lord.
May it be done to me according to your
        word.
R. Alleluia, alleluia.

Gospel: Luke 1:39-45
^{39} Mary set out and traveled to the hill country in haste to a town of Judah, ^{40} where she entered the house of Zechariah and greeted Elizabeth. ^{41} When Elizabeth heard Mary's greeting, the infant leaped in her womb, and Elizabeth, filled with the Holy Spirit, ^{42} cried out in a loud voice and said, "Blessed are you among women, and blessed is the fruit of your womb. ^{43} And how does this happen to me, that the mother of my Lord should come to me? ^{44} For at the moment the sound of your greeting reached my ears, the infant in my womb leaped for joy. ^{45} Blessed are you who believed that what was spoken to you by the Lord would be fulfilled."

Feast of the Holy Family of Jesus, Mary and Joseph

First Reading: Sirach 3:2-6, 12-14

[2] God sets a father in honor over his
        children;
    a mother's authority he confirms
        over her sons.
[3] Whoever honors his father atones for
        sins,
    and preserves himself from them.
When he prays, he is heard;
        [4] he stores up riches who reveres his
        mother.
[5] Whoever honors his father is gladdened
        by children,
    and, when he prays, is heard.
[6] Whoever reveres his father will live a
        long life;
    he who obeys his father brings
        comfort to his mother.

[12] My son, take care of your father when
        he is old;
    grieve him not as long as he lives.
[13] Even if his mind fail, be considerate of
        him;
    revile him not all the days of his life;
[14] kindness to a father will not be
        forgotten,
    firmly planted against the debt of
        your sins
—a house raised in justice to you.

Or 1 Samuel 1:20-22, 24-28

[20] In those days Hannah conceived, and at the end of her term bore a son whom she called Samuel, since she had asked the LORD for him. [21] The next time her husband Elkanah was going up with the rest of his household to offer the customary sacrifice to the LORD and to fulfill his vows, [22] Hannah did not go, explaining to her husband, "Once

the child is weaned, I will take him to appear before the LORD and to remain there forever; I will offer him as a perpetual nazirite."

[24] Once Samuel was weaned, Hannah brought him up with her, along with a three-year-old bull, an ephah of flour, and a skin of wine, and presented him at the temple of the LORD in Shiloh. [25] After the boy's father had sacrificed the young bull, Hannah, his mother, approached Eli and said:

[26] "Pardon, my lord! As you live, my lord, I am the woman who stood near you here, praying to the LORD. [27] I prayed for this child, and the LORD granted my request. [28] Now I, in turn, give him to the LORD; as long as he lives, he shall be dedicated to the LORD." Hannah left Samuel there.

Responsorial Psalm: Psalms 128:1-2, 3, 4-5.

R. (cf. 1) *Blessed are those who fear the Lord and walk in his ways.*

[1] Blessed is everyone who fears the LORD,
    who walks in his ways!
[2] For you shall eat the fruit of your handiwork;
    blessed shall you be, and favored.

R. *Blessed are those who fear the Lord and walk in his ways.*

[3] Your wife shall be like a fruitful vine
    in the recesses of your home;
your children like olive plants
    around your table.

R. *Blessed are those who fear the Lord and walk in his ways.*

[4] Behold, thus is the man blessed
    who fears the LORD.
[5] The LORD bless you from Zion:
    may you see the prosperity of Jerusalem
    all the days of your life.

R. *Blessed are those who fear the Lord and walk in his ways.*

Or Psalms 84:2-3, 5-6, 9-10.

R. (cf. 5a) *Blessed are they who dwell in your house, O Lord.*

² How lovely is your dwelling place, O LORD of
  hosts!
 ³ My soul yearns and pines for the courts
  of the LORD.
My heart and my flesh cry out for the living
  God.
**R. *Blessed are they who dwell in your house, O
  Lord.***
⁵ Happy they who dwell in your house!
  Continually they praise you.
⁶ Happy the men whose strength you are!
  Their hearts are set upon the pilgrimage.
**R. *Blessed are they who dwell in your house, O
  Lord.***

⁹ O LORD of hosts, hear our prayer;
  hearken, O God of Jacob!
¹⁰ O God, behold our shield,
  and look upon the face of your anointed.
**R. *Blessed are they who dwell in your house, O
  Lord.***

Second Reading: Colossians 3:12-21

Brothers and sisters: ¹² Put on, as God's chosen ones, holy and beloved, heartfelt compassion, kindness, humility, gentleness, and patience, ¹³ bearing with one another and forgiving one another, if one has a grievance against another; as the Lord has forgiven you, so must you also do. ¹⁴ And over all these put on love, that is, the bond of perfection. ¹⁵ And let the peace of Christ control your hearts, the peace into which you were also called in one body. And be thankful. ¹⁶ Let the word of Christ dwell in you richly, as in all wisdom you teach and admonish one another, singing psalms, hymns, and spiritual songs with gratitude in your hearts to God. ¹⁷ And whatever you do, in word or in deed, do everything in the name of the Lord Jesus, giving thanks to God the Father through him.

¹⁸ Wives, be subordinate to your husbands, as is proper in the Lord. ¹⁹ Husbands, love your wives, and avoid any bitterness toward them. ²⁰ Children, obey your parents in everything, for this is pleasing to the Lord. ²¹ Fathers, do not provoke your children, so they may not become discouraged.

Or Colossians 3:12-17

Brothers and sisters: [12] Put on, as God's chosen ones, holy and beloved, heartfelt compassion, kindness, humility, gentleness, and patience, [13] bearing with one another and forgiving one another, if one has a grievance against another; as the Lord has forgiven you, so must you also do. [14] And over all these put on love, that is, the bond of perfection. [15] And let the peace of Christ control your hearts, the peace into which you were also called in one body. And be thankful. [16] Let the word of Christ dwell in you richly, as in all wisdom you teach and admonish one another, singing psalms, hymns, and spiritual songs with gratitude in your hearts to God. [17] And whatever you do, in word or in deed, do everything in the name of the Lord Jesus, giving thanks to God the Father through him.

Or 1 John 3:1-2, 21-24

Beloved: [1] See what love the Father has bestowed on us that we may be called the children of God. And so we are. The reason the world does not know us is that it did not know him. [2] Beloved, we are God's children now; what we shall be has not yet been revealed. We do know that when it is revealed we shall be like him, for we shall see him as he is.

[21] Beloved, if our hearts do not condemn us, we have confidence in God [22] and receive from him whatever we ask, because we keep his commandments and do what pleases him. [23] And his commandment is this: we should believe in the name of his Son, Jesus Christ, and love one another just as he commanded us. [24] Those who keep his commandments remain in him, and he in them, and the way we know that he remains in us is from the Spirit he gave us.

Alleluia: Colossians 3:15A, 16A
R. Alleluia, alleluia.
[15A] Let the peace of Christ control your hearts;
[16A] let the word of Christ dwell in you richly.
R. Alleluia, alleluia.

Or cf. Acts 16:14B
R. Alleluia, alleluia.
[14B] Open our hearts, O Lord,
to listen to the words of your Son.
R. Alleluia, alleluia.

Gospel: Luke 2:41-52
[41] Each year Jesus' parents went to Jerusalem for the feast of Passover, [42] and when he was twelve years old, they went up according to festival custom. [43] After they

had completed its days, as they were returning, the boy Jesus remained behind in Jerusalem, but his parents did not know it. 44 Thinking that he was in the caravan, they journeyed for a day and looked for him among their relatives and acquaintances, 45 but not finding him, they returned to Jerusalem to look for him. 46 After three days they found him in the temple, sitting in the midst of the teachers, listening to them and asking them questions, 47 and all who heard him were astounded at his understanding and his answers. 48 When his parents saw him, they were astonished, and his mother said to him, "Son, why have you done this to us? Your father and I have been looking for you with great anxiety." 49 And he said to them, "Why were you looking for me? Did you not know that I must be in my Father's house?" 50 But they did not understand what he said to them. 51 He went down with them and came to Nazareth, and was obedient to them; and his mother kept all these things in her heart. 52 And Jesus advanced in wisdom and age and favor before God and man.

Printed in Great Britain
by Amazon

38548032R00073